THE JOSEPH STORY

Dan and Carol
Grace and blessings to you.
Great visiting this week here
in Decatur.
May God bless you.
Ron & Christi Bishop

THE JOSEPH STORY

Treachery, Betrayal, and Redemption

Ron A. Bishop

RON A. BISHOP

THE JOSEPH STORY

Printed in the USA
Library of Congress Control Number: 2010928858

ISBN: 978-0-9826954-2-5

Cover Design: Joseph & Doryann Rohrs
Front Cover Photograph: Ron Bishop *(Taken in Upper Egypt near the Valley of the Pharaohs.)*
Author Photograph *(Back Cover)*: David Teran | www.davidteran.com

Prepared for Publication By

PALM TREE
PUBLICATIONS

Palm Tree Publications is a Division of Palm Tree Productions
www.palmtreeproductions.net
PO BOX 122 | KELLER, TX | 76244

To Contact the Author:

WWW.THEJOSEPHSTORY.COM

DEDICATION

I would like to acknowledge the rings in my tree by recognizing those who have spoken into my life over the years. These individuals have invested themselves in me and have given a boost to my life and ministry fulfillments. Without them my perspectives and even my theology would have taken on a different pattern. They have woven into my spirit a level of understanding, which has given me strength and vitality. I owe them a huge debt of gratitude. I would like to dedicate this book to my main mentors to acknowledge them and give honor to them.

I have enjoyed six main mentors in my life and ministry. These major mentors have given so much of themselves to me and have genuinely made a difference. I would like to dedicate this book to these "Fathers in Ministry" and thank them for all they gave during the years they invested in me.

- **Earl Daniel Bishop** – *(My Father, Deceased)*
- **Dr. B.J. Pruitt** – Valrico, Florida
- **Rev. David B. Coote** – San Antonio, Texas
- **Pastor M. W. Hazelip** – *(My college teacher, Deceased)*
- **Dr Fred Roberts** – Durban, South Africa
- **Pastor Mack A. Lavine** – *(My closest friend for many years, Deceased)*

These men have influenced my ethics, wisdom, delivery, content when ministering, sense of good judgment, and expanded my paradigms. They have pollinated my thoughts with new ideas and brought balance to my own ideas. I have learned from a full spectrum of perspectives and adjusted my ideals by their speaking into my life. I shall never be the same because of all they gave me.

In addition to these great men there have been several "minor mentors," (minor in the sense of the length of time I spent with them) whose names I shall not give. They have also impacted my life. Some of them do not even realize the impact they made, but I am fully aware of the value they added to me, and my worldview. The impact they made on my life was major and I shall ever be grateful.

ACKNOWLEDGEMENTS

I would like to acknowledge some people who greatly contributed to making this endeavor possible. First of all I wish to thank my family—Christi, my wife of forty years, for typing the manuscript, and for encouraging me to stay vigilant while working on this book. I also wish to thank my son, Cameron Bishop, for his professional advice and my daughter, Doryann Rohrs for her work in designing the cover of this book. I am so proud of my wife, our children, their spouses, and our grandchildren. Thank you for being such a loving part of my life. To our son, Cameron, and his wife, Letha—you have brought to us Cole, Lauren and Trent. To our daughter, Doryann, and her husband, Joseph Rohrs—you have given us Gwynne, Cyrus and Cora Miette. I draw such great strength from every member of my family and could not go without sharing their names with you.

I would also like to acknowledge Jerry and Jana Lackey, the founders of Love Botswana Outreach Mission Trust in Maun, Botswana, which is in the northern part of the Kalahari Desert. Thank you Jerry and Jana for inviting us to help out at Love Botswana for a time. The beautiful missions campus provided a serene, inspirational venue from which to write *The Joseph Story*.

I want to give honor to Pastor Dan and Sharon Cowen, of Parowan, Utah. They also provided an inspirational setting for me to continue writing on the book. Dan and Sharon have always been great friends and encouraged us by making sure we had generous provision and an opportunity to write.

I also wish to thank all my dear friends and partners who gave financially toward this project. Thank you for believing.

ENDORSEMENTS

Ron and Christi Bishop are delightful, dedicated ministers of the good news of Jesus Christ. I have had the honor of being their friend for many years and have seen them in action ministering in foreign countries. One thing has always characterized their life and message; it is the joy of the Lord that springs from their hearts of love and faith. Ron is an insightful scholar of the Word of God as he instructs God's leaders on the continents of the world. This book reflects the scholarship, joy and insights that he has gleaned and it is a spiritual feast for all who desire to understand the secrets of Joseph's fruitful life.

MICHAEL HERRON
President of Mike Herron Music
www.MikeHerronMusic.com

I have had the privilege of knowing Ron Bishop for many years and to count him among my friends. As a teacher of the Bible I can say he's unequivocally among the best. His insights, thoughts and understanding of the Bible as it relates to our time, make him one of the most relevant Bible expositors I've met.

MARCOS WITT

Recording Artist, Founder of Canzion Music Group
Pastor of Spanish Church at Lakewood Church | Houston, Texas, USA
Four-time Latin Grammy Award-winning Christian Singer
www.MarcosWitt.net | www.CanZion.com

Ron has much experience as a Christian leader, functioning as pastor, missions' ambassador, teacher, and evangelist. In his teachings, Ron skillfully uses his experience to bring fresh understanding to the Word of God. His book, *The Joseph Story*, will both inspire and challenge the reader: inspire to a higher walk, and challenge to a greater faith.

DAVID MICHAEL BELL
Lead Pastor of Destiny Church
Recording artist, Founder of Dancing Heart Productions
San Antonio, TX
www.DestinyChurch.cc

The story of Joseph is well known, but by basing his research, not only on the Scriptures, but also on the historical account of Josephus, Ron Bishop brings new insights into Joseph's life. Particularly striking is Ron's observation that it was not only the coat of many colours that was a feature of Joseph's life, but also the coats given to him by Potiphar and Pharaoh. This writing not only contains many valuable lessons for life, it is also a very good read.

BRUCE STREATHER
Attorney and Solicitor, Streathers and Company
London, England, UK
www.Streathers.com

What an action filled book of God's hand at work when all goes ripped. I have known Ron and Christi Bishop for over 30 years, and find *The Joseph Story* reveals God's heart and character of what He is trying to produce within us. This exciting book will confirm God's favor in your life, and will be a great reminder that our destiny, and dreams are always in the hand and heart of God? This is a great read that will challenge you as you grow in character.

HAL SANTOS
Lead pastor at Grace Church
Fairview Heights, Illinois, USA
www.graceweb.tv

Thirty-seven years ago I was a stranger in my own country, having returned from one year of serving with the Marine Corps in Vietnam as a Navy Corpsman. Having difficulty not only relating to other people, but also finding Christians serious about their faith, I one day stumbled across Ron & Christi Bishop in a small country church in Maryland. They reached out at a very critical time helping me get reoriented back into civilian life and grounded in a local community of believers. Their impact was such that I have never let them out of my reach. Their love for the Body of Christ and their passion for Jesus Christ have left an indelible mark on their lives. They lead and point people to Jesus Christ. They don't love and serve with baggage and underlying motives. What they see and teach with clarity and great illustration is Jesus Christ, the Savior of us all. Their life mission is to present Him to all in the world. I am grateful that the Lord orchestrated our friendship many years ago. I heartily endorse Ron and Christi as a couple who will love you where you are and encourage you to pursue Jesus Christ with passion and with purpose.

GARY QUERNEMOEN
Field Operations Manager
Veterans Employment Service
Minnesota Department of Employment & Economic Development.
A Friend

WHY USE DIFFERENT VERSIONS OF THE BIBLE

The Word of God inspires generation after generation to read it, be challenged by it, and make the necessary adjustments to better prepare our lives for this life and eternity. Throughout the centuries, scholars have succeeded in redefining our response to the ancient languages. They have published many versions of the Bible and aided us in better understanding theology as well as the setting for all the stories of the Bible—both Old Testament and New Testament.

"No matter how wonderful a translation is, it has limitations. The Bible was originally written using 11,280 Hebrew, Aramaic, and Greek words, but the typical English translation uses only around 6000 words. Obviously, nuances and shades of meaning can be missed, so it is always helpful to compare translations."[1]

It is my desire to tell the stories of the Bible with clarity to a new generation of reader. The 21st century reader deserves to have books and media productions available to them, which are colorful, diverse, and transparent. I have attempted to bring diversity of communicative skills to a new level by carefully selecting the best words to express a thought. Tradition is good, but a new approach to an old challenge can also serve the reader well.

Therefore, I have tapped into the wealth of ten different versions of the Bible to paint for you the best picture to reveal accurately what took place so many millennia ago.

Endnotes

1. Rick Warren's *The Purpose Driven Life*, Appendix 3, page 325

THE LIFE AND WORKS OF FLAVIUS JOSEPHUS

The Benefits of Merging the Bible and The Life and Works of Flavius Josephus

This book was birthed from the desire to introduce a new generation to the stories of the Christian faith. Too often we long for more details to the credible events of so long ago. It is always my hope to tell the stories of the Bible in a more colorful way.

The Bible is accurate and complete by itself. However, by using the writings of the ancient historians we can get a bigger picture of the events of the day as they unfolded. As the compiler of this fresh look at Joseph, I have attempted to correlate the time worn and thoroughly-tested picture of his life as found in the Holy Scriptures, with the credible 2000 year-old-work of the famed Jewish historian, Flavius Josephus. Josephus does bring to bear many ingredients which would make the stories more exciting and informative to a new generation.

The occasions where the Bible and Josephus seem to conflict are few in number; on those rare occasions I always choose the Bible as the supremely accurate standard.

It is my hope that you will find *The Joseph Story* to be a good read, as well as an inspiring and challenging journey to a stronger faith.

I do sincerely hope that you will find yourself "reading the stories of the Bible like you've never read them before."

—Ron A. Bishop

CONTENTS

FOREWORD

The Joseph Story, as narrated by Ron Bishop, is pleasurable reading with information presented in the best-written text. One has to read the book to appreciate the truths and contents described in this small Foreword.

Every person who has been called of God should read this story. You will find the sufferings of betrayal which will be experienced by those who are the servants of God. You will also see how those we have trusted and loved are often the perpetrators of our suffering.

This book is a manual to be read and spiritually digested. Use it to see beyond suffering and abuse and that God has a plan to fulfill in your life. This author articulates that in the life of Joseph, patience was one of his redeeming features and was the stepping-stone to become governor over all of Egypt.

The Joseph Story also gives warning that blessing and success will often be attacked with jealousy, hatred, and intrigue. This author weaves into the story excellent Biblical advice from his research and writings on the story of Joseph.

"All scripture is given by inspiration of God, and is profitable for doctrine, for reproof, for correction, for instruction in righteousness: That the man of God may be perfect, thoroughly furnished unto all good works" (2 Timothy 3:16-17 KJV).

From the behavior of Jacob's twelve sons, one learns about the carnality that is present in the lives of those that are called to be the chosen of God. Ron Bishop is artistic in the manner in which he displays the behavior of Joseph's brothers. Reconciliation and redemption produces encouragement to all who have been betrayed and severely hurt in their endeavor to serve God.

Actually, I feel that the style and contents of this book warrant being made into a movie. *The Joseph Story*, is not only a Biblical and historical account, it is entertaining as well. A young child and a university professor should enjoy *The Joseph Story* equally.

Ron and Christi Bishop have a passion to strengthen leaders of the Church around the world. Every leader should read *The Joseph Story* prayerfully and then stand strong when evil days come.

"Wherefore take unto you the whole armour of God, that ye may be able to withstand in he evil day, and having done all, to stand" (Ephesians 6:13 KJV).

Don Normand, DD

Prolific Author and Long-Term Pastor

South African by Birth, Residing with his wife, Cindy, in Melrose, FL, USA

Chaplain in the Rhodesian Army

www.BibleSermons.com

PROLOGUE

In the Beginning, Things got Broken ...

Joseph comes to us from a family of broken parts. Warts and all, this family is a powerful part of history and indicative of how the hearts of men have always been character-challenged.

Isaac—Jacob—Joseph

Isaac was Jacob's father. He commissioned his son to go to the family village of his wife, Rebekah, and find a wife from among Laban's daughters. He instructed him not to take a wife from among the local Canaanite women, but instead to choose a wife from among the daughters of his uncle, Laban.[1]

Jacob first met Rachel beside the well. There she was, like she was every other day, watering Laban's sheep. This young and beautiful lady caught his attention. Rachel, the shepherdess, was mesmerizing to Jacob.

This intriguing relationship eventually led to marriage and the birth of Joseph. But this key relationship that would set so much of history in motion was surrounded by much deception, conflict and drama.

The story of Joseph is a heart stopper—a life grabber. It is a narrative which will challenge your life and alter your world-view as much as any other story you will ever encounter. This book is written for the purpose of awakening the dreamer within you, so that you can climb out of any "can't do" attitudes and embrace a "can do" way of thinking.

The Lord was Joseph's source. Faith in God was Joseph's hope. It has been nearly 4000 years since the Joseph Story took place in Egypt, but nothing has changed in the nature of man—both good and bad. Culturally, Joseph's trials may be different in some ways, but as Jeremiah said, "The heart is hopelessly dark and deceitful, a puzzle that no one can figure out. But I, God, search the heart and examine the mind. I get to the heart of the human. I get to the root of things. I treat them as they really are, not as they pretend to be."[2]

In order to fully understand the story of Joseph, it is best to first introduce you to his parents and the facts surrounding his birth.

The story you are about to read brought great stress to Jacob and heartache to each of those involved:

- In the beginning, Jacob agreed to work for seven years for the hand of Rachel in marriage.

- When it came down to honoring their agreement, Laban, the father of the bride, made a switch on Jacob and Rachel's wedding night, and placed Leah, the older sister, into the marriage bed, instead of Rachel.

* As angry as Jacob was, Laban was still able to negotiate with him and made the agreement that he must work seven more years for the hand of Rachel.

* However, if he made the commitment to work the seven years, he could actually consummate the marriage within this same week of his wedding to Leah. This meant that Jacob was married to both Leah and Rachel in the same week.

LABAN WAS A SLY, DECEITFUL OLD TRICKSTER AND GUILTY OF DOUBLE-DEALING FRAUD

* Each member of this family was now holding personal wounds of disappointment. This would show up over and over again in one form or another. Laban was not building strength into his family with all of his misdeeds, but by sowing distrust and selfishness was instead sabotaging all of their future relationships.

* As the years passed, the heartache continued for Rachel. Because she was unable to bear children, she made a decision to give her maid, Bilhah, to Jacob to bear children in her name.[3]

* The contest raced onward, when Leah, after bearing four sons to Jacob, stopped bearing children. She decided that she must not allow Rachel to get the best of her and so gave her maid, Zilpah, to Jacob so that more children could be born, in her name.[4]

Within a few short years and, as a result of all that happened, Jacob was now husband to four women and father of ten sons and only one daughter. From the beginning Jacob's heart had longed only to be joined to Rachel and no other; and yet the years had

3

brought him a different experience. "Rachel was lovely in form and beautiful."[5] Some said that she was stunningly beautiful.[6] He

> RACHEL WAS
> LOVELY IN FORM
> AND BEAUTIFUL

had promised to work for her hand in marriage seven years and had finally fulfilled his vow. The years had passed and not one child had come from their union, although his other wives had given him many children.[7] Jacob and Rachel continued praying that the Lord would open her womb and give her a son.

Then God remembered Rachel; He listened to her and opened her womb. She became pregnant and gave birth to a son and said, "God has taken away my disgrace." She named him Joseph, and said, "May the Lord add to me another son."[8]

Joseph grew into a fine young man. He was close to his father Jacob. The bond between them became stronger and stronger, largely because they had Joseph's mother, Rachel, in common. Joseph observed the dynamics of human failure and personal indiscretions in his family. This helped him form a value system which would benefit him in areas of wisdom for his own life in the years that would follow. The years of serving Laban were finished and off the family went to pursue their own destiny. The departing was not easy, but finally they had succeeded in moving away from the old home encampment of Rebekah's family.

As they traveled along, caravan style, in the direction of Jacob's childhood home, Joseph became aware of the age-old rift between his father and his uncle, Esau. Jacob's entourage had departed from Laban, in Padanaram, and was traveling en route to Shechem, in the land of Canaan,[9] when they heard that Esau, along with an army of 400 men, was coming to meet him. Jacob was frantic with fear. He divided his household, along with the flocks and herds and camels, into two groups; for he said, "If Esau attacks one group, perhaps the other can escape."[10] Joseph was instructed to stay close by his mother, and at the back of the group to which he was assigned. From a distance he could see the two older men as they met. Everyone had expected the worst and Esau was, by no means, trusted by Jacob or his family.

Joseph watched as his father led this entire procession toward Esau and his men. As Jacob approached "he bowed seven times, honoring his brother. But Esau ran and embraced him, held him tight and kissed him. And they both wept."[11]

Esau looked past Jacob and, in a brotherly manner, inquired as he saw the women and children. He asked, "Who are these with you?" So Jacob said, "The children whom God has graciously given your servant."[12]

Joseph watched as Bilhah and Zilpah stepped forward, and their children; all then bowed themselves before Esau and his men; then Leah and her children bowed to give honor to this relative. Finally, Joseph was nudged forward, with his mother, Rachel. They were the last to present themselves and bow.

Joseph could barely hear his father and his Uncle Esau as they spoke of the large drove of livestock, which had been sent ahead of Jacob and his family, to meet Esau. It became apparent that Jacob had sent them ahead as a gift to his estranged brother. Now he could hear Esau's response to Jacob: "Brother, I already have plenty, keep them for yourself."[13] But upon Jacob's insistence Esau did finally accept the generous gift.

Years later Joseph would remember back to how these two men had differences which had lasted many years, and yet they had

THESE TWO MEN HAD DIFFERENCES, WHICH HAD LASTED MANY YEARS, AND YET THEY HAD PROVEN WISE ENOUGH TO LAY THEIR EGOS ASIDE TO RECEIVE EACH OTHER IN LOVE proven wise enough to lay their egos aside to receive each other in love. This became a deposit of wisdom for him to use, should the need arise in his own life.

This family was quite nomadic. They moved several times in his short life and now were uprooting their camp, folding away their tents and setting their sights for another pastureland and yet another new beginning. They were leaving Bethel and heading toward the tower of Edar.[14]

Benjamin is Born, Rachel Dies

The journey was going well, but his mother, Rachel, was experiencing some problems. She was getting closer to delivering another child. Not far into the journey and near the village of Ephrath, she began "hard, hard labor"[15] and gave birth to a son. The midwife tried to comfort her, and said, "Don't be afraid, you have another boy," however, the labor had become so intense that those around her began to fear for her very life. "With her last breath, for she was now dying, she named her son Benoni (*meaning* Son of my Pain)."[16] Everyone was aghast in the moments that followed, as they realized the difficulty, and the curse, this name would bring to this child. They understood why she had uttered this name, but still, how would the child pick up the pieces and face his own life in the future? But for the unfortunate time of his birth, this boy might have been named something better, something proactive. While experiencing both the pains of delivery and the pangs of death, Rachel was unable to think beyond this moment.

Immediately the midwife brought Jacob into the tent. He surveyed the situation and realized that he must settle the future for this twelfth son.

Benjamin was coming into this world with life, while his mother Rachel was leaving this world in death. It was a painful parting, not only for mother and child, but also for those who were nearby. Rachel's death was traumatic and made worse, when from her lips and with her last breath, she had released a name, which would bring thoughts of a curse instead of blessing. Jacob had to decide, promptly, whether he would veto her decision and give his new son a better chance at life, or allow this moment to form a dark cloud, in the minds of each member of this family.

Jacob was swift in his decision to kiss Rachel goodbye and with his next words make the right decision for the boy. He passed the test and said clearly, so as to send a clear message to all: This boy will not be named "Son of Pain,"[17] nor "Son of my Sorrow," but "Son of my right hand."[18]

HE SHALL BE CALLED "SON OF MY RIGHT HAND," LET'S GIVE BENJAMIN A CHANCE

All could hear the low voice of this patriarch as he spoke decisively and with the determination of a judge: "He shall be called Benjamin."[19] The issue was settled.

It is often difficult, especially during times of bereavement to be decisive; especially, if it means opposing the wishes of the loved one who has gone, but Jacob did the right thing for Benjamin and the family.

Rachel, Jacob's beloved, was buried on a stop-over place just outside of a city few have heard of, Ephrath. It will be helpful to know that it was later given a new name, Bethlehem—certainly more familiar. At the time it was the best Jacob could do. This family was in transition and a better place was just not available. This family was a shepherding family and they had to be true to themselves. The seasons were changing and the grazing lands of Bethel were not adequate for the time of year. The grass was much better in the region of the Tower of Edar. This move, though necessary, had now become a time of sadness for the family.

Jacob had loved Rachel so much that he took extra time and effort setting up a monument of stones upon her grave, and it is there to this day.[20] Even in the twenty-first century, Rachel's Tomb is highly regarded and frequently visited. Her tomb is only a short distance from the town, and yet Jacob did not choose to take her into the city, nor carry her on to Hebron, but decided to bury her in the middle of nowhere, on the side of the road. It has been said that Jacob's choice to bury her on a deserted roadside was wise, because it made her tomb available to her many descendants who would eventually be driven from their homes and forced into exile in Babylon. On their march they would pass on this very road, and they would cry to Rachel. Jewish people felt that they could take courage from her presence. Interestingly, through the centuries, women suffering from infertility, in particular, have been known to travel to her tomb to pray.[21] Even the prophet Jeremiah makes his comments on the place of Rachel in their history.[22]

After showing their respect for Rachel the family set out to complete their journey to the Tower of Edar.

Jacob became successful and happy in the Hebron Valley. He was more prosperous than any other of the inhabitants of that country.[23]

Disappointment for Jacob

By the time Joseph was about nine or ten years old, his brother Reuben had already, "defiled his father's bed"²⁴ by going in to "lay with Bilhah, his father's concubine."²⁵ This moral failure of Reuben had taken place just after Rachel had died. Reuben had enjoyed the rights and privileges of being Jacob's firstborn son—until his indiscretion with Bilhah.

After his disappointment with Reuben, Jacob went through a grave struggle dealing with the problems surrounding the rape of his daughter, Dinah, and the reaction by Simeon and Levi. Let me briefly tell this story, so you will fully appreciate the situation Jacob found himself facing.

One day Dinah, daughter of Jacob and Leah, decided to visit some of the local women. She felt reasonably safe, but did not realize the danger she was putting herself in by traveling alone. Before her return to her family she encountered a young man from one of the villages. This man was of the Hivite clan and was named Shechem. He took advantage of Dinah and raped her. Clearly things had gotten out of hand and now he made every attempt to do damage control, as he expressed a strong attraction to this young Hebrew girl. What he did not know was how strongly this Hebrew family felt about sexual purity. Shechem began to woo her by approaching his own father, Hamor, and asking for his help in securing Dinah's hand in marriage. Hamor was an influential chieftain, and traveled to Jacob's home to attempt to make arrangements for marriage. While they were talking about the situation, Jacob's sons (on their way back from the fields) heard what had happened. They were incensed and exploded with rage. They felt such anger that they were ready to raid Shechem's village immediately.

The family negotiations were already in progress, but neither Jacob, nor his family had given any indication of how they felt about the rape. Hamor was inviting Jacob to merge the families and become as one clan. Shechem even said to the Hebrew family, "Please, say yes. I'll pay anything. Set the bridal price as high as you will—the sky's the limit! Only give me this girl for my wife."

The sons of Jacob said, "We could never give our sister to a man who was uncircumcised." They told Hamor that the only condition before they could talk business, was if all his men become circumcised just like them. They told him if he would do this, then they would do what was asked and freely exchange daughters in marriage. However, if the Shechemites were not willing to comply, then they would take their sister and leave.

All the men agreed, so Hamor went to the public square and spoke to the town council. After explaining everything to the council, all the leaders made the decision to comply with the agreement. They were excited about the prospect of bringing the young Hebrew women into their community to choose from for their wives.

The entire city was pleased at the agreement and all the males submitted to circumcision immediately. Three days after the circumcision was taken care of, and when all the men were very sore (and most vulnerable), "two of Jacob's sons, Simeon and Levi, Dinah's brothers, each with his sword in hand, walked into the city, as if they owned the place and murdered every man there. They also killed Hamor and his son Shechem, rescued Dinah from Shechem's house, and left. When the rest of Jacob's sons came on the scene of slaughter, they looted the entire city in retaliation for Dinah's rape. Flocks, herds, donkeys, belongings—everything, whether in the city or the fields—they took. And then they took all the wives and children captive and ransacked their homes for anything valuable."[26]

Jacob said to his two sons, "You've made my name stink to high heaven among the people here, these Canaanites and Perizzites. If they decided to gang up on us and attack, as few as we are we wouldn't stand a chance; they'd wipe me and my people right off the map." Simeon and Levi were unrepentant, and felt justified for all they had done.[27]

"YOU'VE MADE MY NAME STINK TO HIGH HEAVEN AMONG THE PEOPLE HERE"

As a result of this tragic massacre of the Hivites creating safety issues, Jacob felt pressured to totally relocate from this area to Bethel. God caused the people of the neighboring cities to decide not to pursue Jacob and his family, but rather to allow them to quietly pass to Bethel.

This matter became a big problem in the heart of Jacob and resulted in disillusionment between him and his older sons. The failure of Reuben had brought enough distress to the heart of this old patriarch, but after Simeon and Levi had acted out their revenge against Shechem and his family, it was almost more than he could bear.

Joseph, The True Firstborn Son

Jacob was inclined more and more to seeing Joseph as his true firstborn son—for he had truly loved Rachel most from the beginning. Therefore, because of the failures of Reuben, and then Simeon and Levi, Jacob made a decision to elevate Joseph to firstborn status. This is stated clearly in the scriptures, so that we will not fail to realize why these changes were made. "The family of Reuben the firstborn of Israel:[28] Though Reuben was Israel's firstborn, after he slept with his father's concubine, a defiling act, his rights as the firstborn were passed on to the sons of Joseph

11

son of Israel. He lost his 'firstborn' place in the family tree. And even though Judah became the strongest of his brothers and King David eventually came from that family, the firstborn rights stayed with Joseph."[29]

Jacob was a Late Bloomer

Jacob was older than you might think. He left home and came to live at Laban's house when he was about 77 years of age. Soon afterward, he became engaged to Rachel and committed himself to work for seven years as the bride price for her hand in marriage. At the end of this seven years he was given Leah instead; Jacob had consummated his marriage to Leah before he realized that he had been deceived.[30] To settle the dispute which arose between these two men, Laban conceded and secured Jacob's commitment of seven more years of labor for Rachel's hand. At the end of Leah's bridal week, Laban said to Jacob, "If you promise to work for me for another seven years" then "you can have Rachel too."[31] This additional seven-year agreement has been referred to as "Jacob's trouble."[32]

Jacob had been with Laban for a total of fourteen years when Joseph was born.[33] Immediately after Joseph's birth, Jacob entered his final six-year commitment to Laban.[34] This six years period was to build up his assets before leaving with his family. At the point when Jacob separated from Laban, twenty years had passed.[35]

Therefore, all of Jacob's twelve sons and one daughter, Dinah,[36] were born to him and his wives between his own years of 84 and 100. Actually, the first eleven sons and Dinah were born within seven years (Jacob's years of 84 to 91), leaving Benjamin to be born when Jacob was age 100.

Here is how the years came together for Jacob:

- Jacob met Rachel when he was 77.

- Jacob married Leah and Rachel when he was 84.

- Joseph was born when Jacob was 91.

- Benjamin was born and Rachel died when Jacob was 100.

- Joseph was sold into slavery when Jacob was 108.

- When Joseph was age 30 he was transferred from the prison to the palace in Egypt.[37]

- Jacob was 120 years old when his father, Isaac, died. Isaac died at the age of 180.

- Nine years passed (taking them through the seven years of prosperity and two years of the famine) making Joseph age 39 at the point when his family made the move from Canaan to Egypt. This made Jacob 130 years of age.[38]

The Son of Jacob's Old Age

The statement is made that Joseph was the son of Jacob's old age. The deciding factor for the favor which came to Joseph was actually based on the fact that Rachel was the favorite wife of Jacob; and Joseph was her firstborn son. If not, then Benjamin would have replaced Joseph as the son of his old age.[39] This phrase may be better stated that Joseph was the son who was especially devoted to the care of Jacob in his old age. After the death of Rachel, Joseph became his father's special helper in supplying his wants and being an agent between him and his other sons.[40]

Endnotes

1. Genesis 29:15-30
2. Jeremiah 17:9-10 MSG
3. Genesis 30:3-8
4. Genesis 30:9-13
5. Genesis 29:17 NIV
6. Genesis 29:17 MSG
7. Genesis 29:31-30:21
8. Genesis 30:22-23 NIV
9. Genesis 33:18
10. Genesis 32:7-8 TLB
11. Genesis 33:3 MSG
12. Genesis 33:5 NKJV
13. Genesis 33:9 CEV
14. Genesis 35:16-21
15. Genesis 35:17 MSG
16. Genesis 35:17-18 MSG
17. Genesis 35:18 MSG
18. Genesis 35:18 TLB
19. Genesis 35:18
20. Genesis 35:20 TLB
21. Rachel's Tomb. www.chabad.org
22. Jeremiah 31:14-17
23. Josephus, Antiquities, Book 2, 3:1
24. Genesis 49:4
25. Genesis 35:22 KJV
26. Genesis 34:25-29 MSG
27. Genesis 34:30-31 MSG
28. Jacob was renamed Israel, and still was often called Jacob.
29. I Chronicles 5:1-2 KJV
30. Genesis 29:23-25
31. Genesis 29:27
32. Jeremiah 30:7
33. Genesis 30:22-24
34. Genesis 30:25
35. Genesis 31:38
36. Genesis 30:21
37. Genesis 41:46
38. Genesis 47:9
39. Genesis 37:3 KJV
40. Dake's Annotated Reference Bible, Page 36, "K"

Chapter 1

A NEW DAY, AND THE RULES CHANGE

The values system of each member of Jacob's family was growing. They were each embracing the values they would hold to for life. Tests of character would eventually reveal what values were good, and what changes would need to be made.

Joseph was growing in his own moral qualities, but at seventeen, he lacked maturity. Each son was responsible for the tasks necessary to care for the household and the livestock which Jacob owned. Tending sheep was a major responsibility, and Joseph spent a lot of time caring for them. On one occasion, he was out in the fields with his brothers Dan, Naphtali, Gad, and Asher. Joseph reported to his father some of the bad things they were doing.[1] This did not set well with any of his brothers, creating stress and bad feelings between them. This became part of the breakdown of relationships that followed.

Jacob was unaware that any of these attitudes were developing in his family. Even though he was spry and sharp in many ways, we must note that he was already 108 years of age and quite focused on the things that interested him; for example, his attention to Joseph. It was evident that Jacob loved Joseph more than any of his other sons.

Jacob made a coat of many colors for Joseph. This sent a crystal clear signal, bypassing Reuben, and giving this special gift to Joseph—the 11th son in the family line. It showed Jacob's displeasure with all the older sons, and demonstrated favoritism toward the firstborn son of his favorite wife, Rachel.

THE BIRTHRIGHT DOES NOT HAVE TO GO TO THE FIRSTBORN

Throughout history, Jacob has been heavily criticized for having favored Joseph to give him so great an honored place. It must also be considered that with regard to the issue of the birthright, it was tradition that this must be settled long before the father's demise. In Jacob's mind he was taking care of business in an appropriate way.[2] This tradition was an integral part of the culture of their tribal system.

Reuben was undeniably demoted from being the honored firstborn, to a position of lower rank within the family line. There were justifiable reasons for this action on Jacob's part. Eight years earlier, Reuben had committed a horrific indiscretion against his father and against the entire family. He had gone up to the bed of his father's wife, Bilhah.[3] This act of fornication had brought disgrace upon himself and great dishonor to his father. This transgression had left an open wound never dealt with by Jacob. It had been swept aside and not addressed publicly. Everyone knew the full story of what Reuben had done, but there had never been a public hearing where all the family heard Jacob's response. The subject of Reuben's betrayal had become a major blemish against his very integrity; but no one ever spoke about it.

Everyone knew why the coat was given to Joseph, even though it was not declared on the day it was given.[4] It grated against his ten older brothers when Joseph was placed above them all. In effect, the coat explicitly confirmed that Joseph would become the patriarch of this family. It became a constant irritant to a still open wound.

The birthright coat demonstrated the favor Jacob held in his heart for Joseph and the sincere love he had for Rachel. He had worked seven years for her hand in marriage and then watched her die just eight years ago during the birth of Benjamin.

The coat (or long sleeved tunic) has been described as richly ornamented;[5] a coat of many colors;[6] a brightly colored coat;[7] and an elaborately embroidered coat.[8] It brought with it an obvious mark of honor and rank, because Joseph was now the one to whom the birthright would be given. This was a tribal coat usually reserved for a chief and heir.[9]

Although there was plenty of reason for Jacob to favor Joseph as his firstborn, it did not settle with his ten older sons. To quote the Apostle Paul, "everything is permissible—but not everything is beneficial,[10] all things are lawful … but all things are not expedient."[11]

SKELETONS OFTEN LIVE IN CLOSETS, AND GENERALLY STINK A BIT, BECAUSE THEY NEVER FULLY DIE

Without explanation, Jacob's decision to award the birthright to a younger son, brought confusion to the hearts of his family. The term "skeleton in the closet" refers to unresolved conflict. When a family refuses or neglects to address uncomfortable issues and failures, walls are erected, and relationships are damaged. When Joseph's brothers realized that their father loved him more than them, they grew to hate him—they wouldn't even speak to him.[12] Sibling rivalry grew to its worst levels in this family.

Although Jacob could justify his reasons for giving the coat of birthright to Joseph, the timing created an overwhelming breakdown in the family's unity. The family understood clearly that the coat was linked to the acknowledgement of Joseph as the patriarch of the family, but it angered the older brothers. What they saw more clearly was favoritism. This produced jealousy.

Quite naturally, Joseph enjoyed the favor of his father. It was during this time that he began to have dreams, which spoke of a divine favor, even above that of his family. He was blind to the reactions taking place all around him. He failed to detect the social landmines, which were evident anytime he came near to his brothers. Because of this, he failed to discern danger.

The first dream came to Joseph in the night and left him with real excitement, which he candidly shared with his brothers. He said, "Listen to this dream I had. We were all out in the field gathering bundles of wheat. All of a sudden my bundle stood straight up and your bundles circled around it and bowed down to mine." His brothers said, "So! You're going to rule us? You're going to boss us around? And they hated him more than ever, because of his dreams and the way he talked."[13]

This dream was prophetic. It foretold of how the whole family would be in Egypt during the famine. However, all they could grasp was that Joseph (in receiving the coat from their father) had also been the recipient of the family birthright. This provoked rivalry and jealousy in their hearts. They were jealous for Reuben's sake and for their own loss of being favored less than their kid brother.

A divine destiny was at work in this story. Joseph had much to learn before he would be fully prepared for the enormous responsibilities ahead. God had an assignment for Joseph and it was imperative that he begin the long journey so that he could be introduced to all those who were to be the players in the next chapters of his life. This journey to Egypt would be a one-way trip without hope of return for nearly forty years. The dreams, in conjunction with the weak character of Joseph's brothers, became useful tools to help bring together God's plan.

This first dream was a further reminder that Joseph believed he would have dominion over his brothers and indeed, the authority to reign over them.[14] The brothers felt that there would be no peace in this family if Joseph continued to be in such a place of honor.[15]

The second dream was even more intimidating to these men. Joseph was blind to their hatred, and confidently shared his dreams not only with them, but also with his father, Jacob. "Listen, I had another dream, and this time the sun and moon and eleven stars bowed down to me."[16] Now, Jacob became aware of a possible turmoil within his family. He rebuked him. "What is this? Shall I indeed, and your mother and brothers come and bow before you?"[17]

The first dream confirmed Joseph as the patriarch among his brothers, but the second dream placed him as a ruler over the land and even over his father. It was acceptable within the tradition of their culture for Joseph to see himself as the birthright patriarch over the family clan, but this new dream elevated him to a new level as a king.[18]

All sorts of things were happening in this family:

- The coat had activated sibling rivalry;

- The first dream had accentuated Joseph's new role as the head of the family, as the birthright would do;

- Jacob was now a bit uneasy as Joseph's second dream suggested that he was being given more authority than commonly afforded by the birthright;

- In the natural order of things it looked like Joseph was getting out of control.

It was evident that Joseph's brothers were jealous[19] and envied him.[20] His father gave it quite a bit of thought and wondered, what it all meant.[21]

The level of open communication between each member of Jacob's family seemed to break down more and more with every passing day. The dreams had become the final test of family peace. As a result, all that the ten brothers could think about was getting away. They just wanted to leave home and breathe different air. They didn't want to listen to any more about Joseph, or his dreams, or the birthright.

Dreams are a powerful part of our lives. Some dreams fill us with hopes and aspirations. These often come from daydreams and ignite ideas of a brighter future. Other dreams come to us as night visions[22] and leave us with a state of wonderment. These night visions are usually filled with a little mystique and intrigue, because they remove some of our natural limitations and thrust us into the fantasy of total success.

SOMETIMES OUR DAYDREAMS TAKE WINGS IN OUR NIGHT VISIONS

It is always questionable as to how much of our dreams we should share with those closest to us. Often, our dream confession becomes food for a good laugh or a raised eyebrow, but seldom is taken as seriously or as sacredly as we had hoped. Usually we're left with the idea that maybe we should have kept it to ourselves and waited for the fulfillment instead. To tell such night visions is perhaps our way, without realizing it, of seeking certification, validation, or even affirmation and approval.

It is a challenge for anyone to share their dreams with family. In Joseph's case this was especially true, because he was seen as just one of the siblings, certainly not as a kingly sort!

As long as time remains, nothing will change in this arena. We have to strike a balance between when we should keep quiet, and when we must risk sharing our intimate hopes and dreams. This decision depends on where we need to go and how we're to get there. It just may be that those with whom we share our dreams are meant to be a part of the working process that lies ahead for us to fulfill our destiny. No matter the response of those around you, God has a plan for you. His work in you and through you will be perfect and complete, just as it was with Joseph. May God bless you as you embrace your own journey.

NO MATTER
THE RESPONSE
OF THOSE
AROUND YOU,
GOD HAS
A PLAN FOR YOU

Endnotes

1. Genesis 37:2 TLB
2. Genesis 35:22
3. 1 Chronicles 5:1-2
4. Genesis 37:3 NIV
5. Genesis 37:3 KJV
6. Genesis 37:3 TLB
7. Genesis 37:3 MSG
8. Dake's Annotated Reference Bible, Page 36, "L"
9. 1 Corinthians 10:23 NIV
10. I Corinthians 10:23 KJV
11. Genesis 37:4 MSG
12. Genesis 37:6-8 MSG
13. Genesis 37:8 KJV
14. Genesis 37:8 NIV
15. Genesis 37:11 NIV
16. Genesis 37:10 TLB
17. Genesis 37:8 TLB
18. Genesis 37:11 NIV
19. Genesis 37:11 KJV
20. Genesis 37:11 TLB
21. Daniel 7:7 KJV

Chapter 2

TWENTY PIECES
OF SILVER

After a short while, Joseph's brothers took their father's flocks to Shechem to graze them.[1] Shechem was a country known as being good for feeding cattle. After a time, having been given limited information about their plans, Jacob became melancholy.[2] He even grew suspicious about how his ten sons were doing. He was worried about them, especially in light of all that had happened in the days just before they left.

Jacob was bothered, more and more, by the concerns that his sons had not sent back word from their journeys. Were they safe? When would they return to their home? Some of the thoughts that likely went through his mind were thoughts of their general disposition when they had begun their journey. Were they beset by what had gone on just before they left their camp? Secretly, he must have felt a personal need for reassurance. He wanted his family to be whole. It is likely that he wondered how his sons had received Joseph's dreams and his decision to appoint Joseph as the patriarch over his older brothers. Even though it probably would not change a thing, the fact remained that he really did want to know how they received it all.[3]

Jacob sent Joseph to look for the brothers. He traveled from Hebron to Shechem and searched throughout the countryside for his brothers and their flocks of sheep. After a while a local resident noticed him wandering in the fields and asked him who he was looking for. He responded that he was looking for his brothers and their flocks. Joseph replied, "Have you seen them?" "Yes. They are no longer here. I heard your brothers say they were going to Dothan."[4]

Why Dothan and not Shechem?

Jacob sent Joseph to Shechem, but the sons of Jacob had relocated to Dothan.

God would not allow Joseph to meet up with his murderous brothers in Shechem, because they would not have Egypt and slavery as the options to consider. However, in Dothan there was a major trade route—a natural highway straight to Egypt. Arab merchants traveled this route through Dothan on a daily basis. Dothan was the perfect meeting place for their family reunion.

His brothers activated Joseph's destiny, even if their motives were wrong. It has been said, "God is the final arbiter of history." These brothers did what they did, but in the final analysis of things, God was always in charge. The Lord was looking out for Joseph. All of the events, which were about to take place, were set in motion by God. He orchestrated the

EVEN WITH WRONG MOTIVES, JOSEPH'S BROTHERS ACTIVATED HIS DESTINY sequence so that all the parties involved acted in order for the plan of God to be fulfilled.

Joseph continued his journey to connect with his brothers. He was aware that decisions must be made from conditions found in the field, so he was not put off by their move to the new location of Dothan. After some time he arrived in the area and followed his instinct to find his family.

When Joseph was a long distance away from his brothers, even before he came near them, they conspired against him to kill him. Then they said to one another, "Look, this dreamer is coming![5] Let's kill him and throw him into one of these old cisterns,[6] and we will say, some wild beast has devoured him.[7] Then we'll see what comes of his dreams."[8]

"When Reuben heard this, he tried to rescue him from their hands. 'Let's not take his life,' he said, 'don't shed any blood. Throw him into this cistern here in the desert, but don't lay a hand on him.'" Reuben said this because he intended to rescue Joseph from them and take him back to his father.[9]

Reuben continued to persuade his brothers. He reminded them that wherever a man is, so is God. Their consciences would never let them rest, even to the point that their consciences would seem like their enemies, because they could not be avoided. "Everyone knows that murder is an evil thing to do, so if you kill your brother, then you will be guilty of taking the life of an innocent man, because Joseph has done nothing wrong, and deserving of death."[10]

Reuben did not blame Joseph for being passed over in the family hierarchy. He blamed himself, because of his own failure. Reuben did not want to kill Joseph. As the firstborn son, he was angry and disappointed when his father had passed over him and given the honored coat to Joseph. But he also realized that he was at least partly to blame for his father choosing Joseph. If he had not, in the folly of youthful lust and passion, defiled his father's bed; his father would have had no reason to elevate Joseph.

Like his brothers, Reuben was also jealous of Joseph. He recognized that his own actions made him the most responsible for the way things had played out. Therefore, he must not become a party to murdering Joseph. Reuben realized he could never undo the sins of his past. Perhaps things would work out better for him in the future if he (at least) did nothing else to possibly incur Jacob's wrath, or for that matter, the wrath of God.

Dealing with problems when angry, bitter, and filled with resentment never makes you feel better for very long. These brothers thought they would feel better after removing the dreaded birthright coat. The problem was not the birthright, however, because that was a tradition they recognized as valid. The root of the problem was the jealousy they felt for Joseph, because he was so favored while in his youth.

Ruthless hatred was the spirit of everything that took place in the camp of Joseph's brothers. Upon arriving in the camp there was no happy reunion of family—no smiles, no welcome greetings. Instead there were gruff, intolerant, and hateful words. If Joseph had only imagined the hostility he was about to face, he would have fled from this camp.

ANGER, HATRED, JEALOUSY AND RESENTMENT ARE THE BREEDING GROUNDS FOR MURDER

Anger, hatred, jealousy, and resentment are the breeding grounds for murder. This was the mood of Joseph's brothers and there would not soon be an apology.

Joseph approached the family camp, too late detecting that there was extreme hostility towards him. Before he ever arrived they had been discussing his coming. The first hint of danger he noticed was when several of his brothers approached him and without warning, grabbed his arms and legs, pulling him off the donkey he was riding. The next thing Joseph felt was the removal of his coat as they ripped and extracted it from him, revealing the intent to do him harm.

Joseph had never before felt rejection or even disfavor. He had always felt secure in his place with his family. Yet now, all this had changed in an instant. He experienced terror as he was knocked down several times, jostled between the brothers, and finally dropped into a dry cistern, or pit, which was at the edge of the camp.

Joseph's fall was hard and painful. It had all happened so quickly that he had been taken totally by surprise. At first he looked up from the floor of the dry cistern to see all the faces of his brothers looking down at him. A few moments later and their faces were gone, as they had moved to a sitting area of their camp to continue eating their meal.

JOSEPH'S FALL WAS HARD AND PAINFUL

Pits were often hand dug along the desert highways to catch the surface runoff of rain. This was so that thirsty travelers could have access to water as they traveled. This particular one seemed to have a fault and was a broken cistern,[11] and unable to hold the water as it seeped into the soil beneath.

There are numerous pits or cisterns still to be found in Palestine. They were often hewn out of solid rock, being narrower at the mouth than at the bottom. It would be almost impossible for one to get out of such a pit unaided. Some were even used as dungeons for prisoners.[12]

About the time these brothers sat down, Reuben left the camp, as he had planned, to go on a scouting trip to find more pastureland for the grazing of the sheep. He was confident in his heart that Joseph was safe enough in the pit.[13] Joseph could hear them talking, but could not comprehend exactly what they were saying. These cisterns were generally three to four meters (eight to twelve feet) deep. It was just too high for a man to escape without help. So there he sat—waiting and hoping—realizing that he was weak, injured, vulnerable, and alone. Only God could help him now. If only his father, Jacob, were here, but no, he was far away in the "vale of Hebron"[14] and unaware of any harm that was coming to him.

Judah was in deep thought as he mused over the developing situation regarding his kid brother, Joseph. He sat there at the campfire considering the various ways they could approach their dilemma. Judah did not think of himself as an evil man, even though he had felt murder in his own heart against Joseph. It was a fact that he did have some deeply settled character flaws, which occasionally clouded his mind and kept him from doing what was right. As Judah mused on how to handle this situation, he thought about how his brother, Reuben, had fought to keep Joseph alive. Perhaps his opinion should be considered. After all, he was the oldest of the brothers and had suffered the greater loss when Joseph had been so honored. If they kill him, then they are left without options, so better the choice to keep him alive and let this crisis play itself out.

Judah spoke out, saying, "What are we going to get out of killing our brother and concealing the evidence? Let's sell him to the Ishmaelites, but let's not kill him—he is, after all, our brother, our own flesh and blood."[15]

Judah had calculated that it would be a profitable thing to transact business with these traveling merchants. The merchants would get a slave for resale in Egypt, and the family would be short one big headache. To Judah and his brothers, it seemed like a "win-win" situation.

SELLING JOSEPH— THE MERCHANTS GET A SLAVE FOR RESALE AND THE FAMILY GETS RID OF A BIG HEADACHE— A WIN-WIN SITUATION

This story puts Judah, Leah's fourth born son, at the forefront of this drama. Because his personal fingerprints were on how this story plays out, he found himself in a particularly difficult place of being viewed as the ringleader or principal conspirator in this treachery. It is interesting to see how God deals with him in the end.

The next thing Joseph experienced was when his brothers lowered a rope down inviting him, even coaxing him, to allow them to pull him out and up to safety. Strange, he must have thought, for their behavior now was almost warm and kind, as if they had changed their hearts.

Joseph took hold of the rope and allowed them to pull him out of the pit. Immediately, he could see camels and even several strange men in the camp. In moments they were talking back and forth with Judah and all the brothers; then examining him as if to see the wounds from the beating and rough treatment they'd given him. There seemed to be some disagreement and then the strangers paid them "twenty pieces of silver."[16]

Joseph was sold for twenty pieces of silver. This price is considered, by some, to be the price of a crippled slave. The

JOSEPH WAS THROWN INTO THE PIT—

WHEN GOODS ARE DAMAGED IT AFFECTS THE SELLING PRICE

full price of a healthy slave in that time would have been about thirty pieces of silver. It is apparent that if these brothers had taken better care of their slave, then they could have commanded a better price.

The brothers turned back to their bread while the merchants tugged on the rope which had been tied to Joseph's wrists. He looked back, but the brothers had quickly focused their attention to the camp where they were sitting. In minutes Joseph's view of the camp became faint and distant.

The terror of having been stripped of his coat, beaten by his family, dropped into a pit, then sold into slavery was more than Joseph could ever have imagined for himself.

It was difficult for him to watch his brothers turn their backs toward him. It had been horrifying to feel the blows of their fists as they had beaten him and kicked him. He could see the hatred in their eyes as they ripped, tore, and pulled his coat, which had been so lovingly designed by his father, from his back. Now it was destroyed by venomous disdain from the ones who should have cared. The thing that bothered him most was the look of murder in their eyes—a look that had chilled him to the bone.

BETRAYAL IS ONLY ONE SIDE OF THE COIN—

IN TIME GOD WILL REVEAL THE OTHER SIDE OF THAT SAME COIN

Although Reuben had been among the brothers when Joseph arrived in the camp, Joseph remembered well how he had been the only one to speak up for him and had actually begged for his blood not to be shed. He had seen that Reuben was noticeably absent when he had been pulled from the pit. Joseph would never know the anguish Reuben felt when he returned from his scouting trip to find the pit empty. He would not know the disappointment Reuben felt because he could not rescue Joseph and restore him back to Jacob. When he discovered that Joseph was missing, he tore his clothes in grief. Then he went back to his brothers and lamented, "The boy is gone! What will I do now?"[17]

Reuben had fully intended to rescue Joseph from the pit and safely transport him back to his father. If his brothers had not realized Reuben's intentions before, they surely did now. Two pieces of silver would have been Reuben's share of the bounty after the sale of their brother. Reuben must have glared at those two small coins in his hand as he compared their value to the worth of his younger brother. Perhaps he thought about his father's personal loss, and even about the dreams which Joseph had shared.

One of Joseph's brothers had made a statement just as he was about to enter their camp, "We shall see what will become of his dreams."[18] This comment is a question put in the form of a statement. History would bear out that, in fact, Joseph's dreams were not just the longings of a young dreamer, but rather prophecies of divine origin.

The value of life had escaped these brothers. Joseph was, as far as they had hoped, gone forever. They fully predicted that they would never see his face again. One of the brothers stepped over to the flock, singled out a kid of the goats,[19] and roughly slit its throat with a knife. He then, in one movement and without hesitation, dipped, and spattered its blood on Joseph's coat.[20] This act of slaying the goat reflected a true spirit of premeditation being carried out. After much discussion these brothers stooped very low and were, for now, without remorse.

These men made a vow of secrecy among themselves. Then they took the coat to their father and asked him to identify it. "We found this in a field... is it Joseph's coat or not?" Their father recognized it at once. Jacob began to weep and said, "Yes it is my son's coat. A wild animal has eaten him. Joseph is without doubt torn in pieces."[21]

Then Jacob tore his clothes, put on sackcloth and mourned for his son many days.[22] Jacob sank to a very low place of mourning. His grief was as severe, ".... as if he had been the father of no more than one, without taking any comfort in the rest."[23] Time did not diminish his grief, so the years seemed to bring no relief to Jacob.

Jacob absolutely, "... refused to be comforted" and said, "... in mourning will I go down to the grave to my son."[24]

Endnotes

1. Genesis 37:12 TLB
2. Josephus, Antiquities, Book 2, 2:4
3. Josephus, Antiquities, Book 2, 2:4
4. Genesis 37:17 TLB
5. Genesis 37:18-19 NKJV
6. Genesis 37:20 MSG
7. Genesis 37:20 NKJV
8. Genesis 37:20 NIV
9. Genesis 37:21 NIV
10. Josephus, Antiquities, Book 2, 3:1
11. Jeremiah 2:13
12. Jeremiah 38:6; See also Jeremiah 14:3; Zechariah 9:11, Psalm 28:1, and Dake's Bible, Page 37, "B"
13. Genesis 37:29-30
14. Genesis 37:14 KJV
15. Genesis 37:26-27 MSG
16. Genesis 37:28 KJV
17. Genesis 37:29-30 NLT
18. Genesis 37:20 KJV
19. Genesis 37:31 KJV
20. Genesis 37:31 TLB
21. Genesis 37:33 TLB
22. Genesis 37:34 NIV
23. Josephus, Antiquities, Book 2, 3:4
24. Genesis 37:34 NIV

The Joseph Story

Chapter 3

A Long Walk to His New Home

Joseph made the journey from Dothan to Egypt on foot. This took perhaps as much as a month. His value was not considered in human terms, but only as a monetary asset. Joseph had never been away from his family before so this was especially difficult for him. He was left without any options. In the natural way of thinking, he could see no means of escape or chance of ever being reunited with his father.

There was, however, one bright spot in all of this. Joseph seemed well aware of some underlying divine plan for his life. It was too early for him to fully understand, nevertheless, he would keep his attitude right and his faith strong so that he would be prepared for whatever plan God had for him. Joseph's memory of those dreams would remain with him and continue to be a source of encouragement.

Armed Guards protected Joseph's trip to Egypt. Although Jacob was not nearby and in charge of how the details would go for him, Joseph did not need to worry about survival or

PIRATES AND THIEVES COULD NOT HAVE HARMED JOSEPH AS HE AND HIS SLAVE MASTERS TRAVELED ACROSS THE DESERT

neglect in any way. He need not be concerned for matters like safety, favor, privilege, destiny, or even open doors. These matters were never *only* the responsibilities of Jacob or those who loved him. Here are the words of the Lord God on the subject with regards to any and all of those of us who put their trust in Him: "I know the plans I have for you; plans to prosper you and not to harm you; plans to give you hope and a future."[1]

"I know what I'm doing. I have it all planned out—plans to take care of you, not abandon you, plans to give you the future you hope for."[2]

If Joseph had been worried about what would happen to him in this strange and foreign land of Egypt it was without warrant. He was centered right in the will of God from the moment of his birth throughout all the difficulties and conflicts, slavery, betrayal, and even imprisonment. The Lord was with him because, although at times he may not have seen treachery and betrayal coming his way, his character remained flawless and his heart pure. While those around him were jealous, envious, or even murderous, he was continually in the palm of God's hand and being favored at all times.

Even when Joseph stood alone and vulnerable on the platform of the slave market, God was so fully in charge that no one but Potiphar could have picked him out for purchase.

God had a man. The Lord had a plan, and if Joseph kept a right heart, even hell itself could not soil or damage his up and coming appointment as Prime Minister over Egypt.

Yes, there may have been other ways for Joseph to make his transition from Canaan to Egypt, but this was God's way. The trade route that went through Dothan may have seemed well traveled enough, but it was often inhabited by thieves and robbers. The Midianite merchants were instruments of the Lord to provide for him safe passage.

Anyone who chose this highway was taking a chance that they would be robbed or even killed before reaching their destination. It took a special kind of people and well armed guards to even get the merchants and their assets safely to Egypt. Joseph was, no doubt, heavily protected and in no danger as he made the journey. Oh, the conditions may have been inhumane, and the treatment may have seemed unacceptable, but it really did awaken this immature and naïve boy to the real world.

JOSEPH WAS UNTESTED—
THE CHALLENGES AHEAD WOULD DO HIM GOOD

Joseph had lived in a protective cocoon. He was so nurtured and comfortable that he really did need to be (at least slightly) bruised and badgered. He was of excellent character, but untested and unproven. Even God will not pave your way with gold and rose pedals just because you're His chosen. He will send you through "Boot Camp" or "Basic Training." Like a weapon which has never been used, how can the outcome be sure unless and until it has been tried in the theater of battle? All the ill treatment of Joseph was not unreasonable given the high and lofty position he was to occupy. It was necessary to his preparation.

It would have been out of character for a young Hebrew boy like Joseph to have just made a decision to strike out on his own. To act similarly to the prodigal and make a move to the big city in Egypt was unheard of in that day. Even if he had done this, he would have lacked the contacts to connect him to his destiny. It is ludicrous to imagine any other means for Joseph to get to pagan Egypt, the very place where he would need to be thirteen years later to meet Pharaoh, and then be in perfect sequence with God's timetable.

After many days of walking, the desert sands gave way to the more firmly packed streets of an Egyptian city. There were more people in this place than Joseph had ever seen. He was immediately aware of different accents, along with strange and different smells. He was intrigued with the market atmosphere, the animals, and finally even the slave market. Oh, how he would have enjoyed looking around, inspecting all that his senses were discovering, but he was also aware that his hands were tied and that he was being pulled along (probably behind a camel or other slaves). Joseph had no freedoms, no human rights, and no personal choices. It was a difficult discovery, but he saw his level of value and his degree of freedom to be about the same as that of a donkey. He was no longer his own, but rather the property of a stranger who refused to even consider holding a conversation with him. As far as his slave masters were concerned, the human slaves were no more able to engage in meaningful conversation than a donkey.

Soon after arriving in this city, Joseph was ushered into the market place, and paraded up onto a dirty platform along with many others from far away places. Joseph was unaware of the evaluation system of this slave market. He knew nothing of how he would be cared for or who would consider choosing him for purchase. He only did as he was told—stand up straight; do not look into the eyes of those who will examine you, and do not attempt to speak. He obeyed as best he could.

There was one man who fastened his gaze on Joseph and recognized him for his intellect and abilities. He quickly made the arrangements and the purchase was done. Joseph knew nothing of this man or what his assignment was to be. Later he would find out his name was Potiphar. In moments he found himself leaving all those surroundings and going deeper into the city, into a residential area with big and beautiful homes.

THE PURCHASE WAS MADE— A NEW SLAVE JOINED EGYPT'S HUMAN TRAFFICKING WORLD

Upon arrival he was placed under the charge of the man responsible for all the slaves owned by Potiphar, the master of this huge household. Joseph was later able to learn that Potiphar was a member of the personal staff of Pharaoh, the King of Egypt. The Lord greatly blessed Joseph there in the home of his master, so that everything he did succeeded.[3] When his master saw that the Lord was with him and that the Lord gave him success in everything he did, Joseph found favor in his eyes,[4] and was appointed to be Potiphar's personal aide. There were many facets to his new responsibilities. As a result, Joseph became the administrator over all the governmental and personal enterprises of Potiphar. This included everything he owned at home and in the fields. This reduced Potiphar's major decisions to basically choosing what he would eat when his meal times came around.[5]

Potiphar had a number of titles and responsibilities. He was Pharaoh's Chief Executioner, Captain of the King's Bodyguard, and was responsible for the oversight of the King's prison. In effect, Potiphar was the Chief of Police.[6] If anyone offended

Pharaoh, it was the duty of such guards to destroy the offender, and that without giving him a trial. He was to take care of Pharaoh and to execute his will on all subjects of his displeasure. It is reasonable to conclude, as the prison was under the jurisdiction and responsibility of Potiphar, that Joseph would have included its oversight in his official duties. This would have given him occasion to become acquainted with the prison warden, or keeper of the prison.

Therefore, it would seem natural that the keeper of the prison longed to have a man such as Joseph as his own personal aide to assist him in administrating the prison. Joseph was good at making friends and this would serve him well.

Potiphar held Joseph in such respect that he taught him many things, which would normally be available to him only if he were a free man, even to the point that he could eat a higher level of diet than what is generally allotted to slaves.[7] Because he kept his heart right and trusted the Lord to go before him, the favor of God would follow Joseph from one life chapter to the next.

Endnotes

1. Jeremiah 29:11 NIV
2. Jeremiah 29:11 MSG
3. Genesis 39:1-2 TLB
4. Genesis 39:3-4 NIV
5. Genesis 39:3-6
6. Genesis 39:1 TLB
7. Josephus, Antiquities, Book, 4:1

Chapter 4

THE BOSS'S WIFE

Joseph was a strikingly handsome young man. As time went on, his master's wife became infatuated with him and one day said, "Sleep with me."[1] Potiphar's wife was confident that if she made her desires known to Joseph, "… she could easily persuade him to come and lie with her, and that he would look upon it as a piece of happy fortune… that she would like him so much as to give him the privilege of her favor."[2]

Joseph refused. "Look, my master trusts me with everything in the entire household; he himself has no more authority here than I have! He has held back nothing from me except you yourself because you are his wife. How can I do such a wicked thing as this? It would be a great sin against God."[3]

She pestered him day after day after day, but he stood his ground. He refused to go to bed with her,[4] and kept out of her way as much as possible. Then one day as he was in the house going about his work—as it happened, no one else was around at the time—she came and grabbed him by the sleeve

41

demanding, "Sleep with me." He tore himself away, but as he did, his jacket slipped off and she was left holding it as he fled from the house. When she saw that she had his jacket, and that he had fled, she began screaming; and when the other men around the place came running in to see what had happened, she was crying hysterically. "My husband had to bring in this Hebrew slave to insult us!" she sobbed. "He tried to rape me, but when I screamed, he ran, and forgot to take his jacket." She kept the jacket, and when her husband came home that night, she told him her story. "That Hebrew slave you've had around here tried to rape me, and I was saved by my screams. He fled, leaving his jacket behind!"[5]

> JOSEPH SLIPPED RIGHT OUT OF HIS COAT—
>
> SHE COULD HOLD HIS COAT, BUT SHE WOULD NOT GET HIM

Joseph lived his life in such a way that kept him always vigilant, on alert, and prepared to do the right thing. He knew that his destiny was in the hands of God and that God required his children to maintain a high moral conduct. He also realized that Satan is always up to no good and will try to slip his net over you when you're least expecting it. Joseph knew that only God was fully aware of why he was living in Egypt. Just like the coat he had been given by his father so long ago, he knew that, in some way, this coat was also a symbol of his position, or standing. His coat was not fastened. If someone really wanted to take his coat from him, they could do so without getting him as well.

> SATAN IS ALWAYS UP TO NO GOOD, AND WILL TRY TO SLIP HIS NET OVER YOU, WHEN YOU'RE LEAST EXPECTING IT

When Potiphar's wife took a firm hold of his sleeve, Joseph just slipped out of his coat. His movement was smooth and without jerks or hesitation. Before she fully realized what had happened, Joseph was down the hall and out the door.

Upon hearing her account of what had happened, Potiphar was furious. He ordered that Joseph be imprisoned—the same prison where the King's prisoners were kept in chains.[6]

Although falsely accused, Joseph refused to fight for his rights. He did not defend himself against the accusations of Potiphar's wife for at least one of three reasons:

* He was a slave and had NO RIGHTS so his defense was not even considered. Potiphar may not have come face to face in close range, but ordered him from across the court, therefore eliminating any personal contact and thus, reaffirming the low state of a slave.

* To accuse his master's wife of a crime was almost the same as if he had accused the master himself of one. He may have received the death penalty if he had dared to attack her character in any way.

* Joseph trusted God. He did not wish to fight his own battles, but rather to leave them to God, who was more able to make everything right in the end. God was, "... more powerful than those that inflicted the punishment upon him."[7]

Endnotes

1. Genesis 39:6-7 TLB
2. Josephus, Antiquities, Book 2, 4:2
3. Genesis 39:8-9 TLB
4. Genesis 39:10 MSG
5. Genesis 39:10-18 TLB
6. Genesis 39:20 TLB
7. Josephus, Antiquities, Book 2, 5:1

Chapter 5

SPENDING TIME IN THE BIG HOUSE

Joseph was arrested and taken as a criminal from the court
of Potiphar to the prison. A grave cloud hung over him in
the minds of all those who saw what was happening in his life.
Whether guilty or innocent, there would be no trial, and therefore
no chance of acquittal. Only time would tell what had really
happened and who had been guilty of evil designs. The favor
and respect in the heart of Potiphar for Joseph was on hold (and
perhaps even worse) against the backdrop of his wife's wailing.
This was not the time for discussion. Now was not the time for
defense. As hard as it seems, sometimes it is best to remain quiet
and allow a higher power to weigh the balances of guilt and
innocence.

Favor often comes from the most unlikely places, and so it was
that the jailer felt a respect for Joseph and showed him kindness.
It became obvious that the Lord was with Joseph in the prison
and caused the jailer to respond favorably to him. In fact, he soon
handed over the entire prison administration to Joseph, so that all

the other prisoners were responsible to him. This prison and this "chief jailer had no more worries after that, for Joseph took care of everything, and the Lord was with him so that every detail ran smoothly and well."[1]

The keeper of the prison[2] or prison warden[3] was already a part of Joseph's network of friends and acquaintances. As Potiphar's personal aide, he had already been overseeing this prison. He had likely visited this prison many times before his arrest and had become well acquainted with him. This certainly benefited Joseph.

Prison life for Joseph was certainly not as good as walking freely in Potiphar's employ, but still it was not so bad for him. He had immediately been shown special favor and was granted privileges uncustomary for normal prison life. Joseph was even invited to eat a better diet than the rest of the prisoners.[4]

It is not clear just how many years Joseph served in Potiphar's home or how many years he served in the prison, respectively, but combined, it came to a total of thirteen years. It spanned the entire time from when he was sold into slavery to when he was brought before Pharaoh to interpret his dreams.[5]

Day by day Joseph conscientiously cared for his fellow prisoners and saw his work as an opportunity to serve without resentment. He refused to be discouraged by the present circumstances, which would have defeated men of weaker constitution. He gave his best care to every situation and faithfully did it with dignity.[6]

Some time later, a day came to Potiphar that would change his life in so many ways. It began as a normal day, but when Potiphar arrived at Pharaoh's palace on this day, he found circumstances to be quite sensitive. The mood of Pharaoh was explosive, because of something the chief cupbearer (or chief butler)[7] and the chief baker[8] had done. It is obvious that their offense had something to do with the food services, because of their roles within the palace. It is clear that they had offended[9] Pharaoh in some significant way.

Potiphar had responded, as he always did, by stepping in as the Captain of the Guard. His responsibility was to make sure that the offenders were quickly taken from the King's view and dealt with swiftly, and outside of public view.

> POTIPHAR HANDED OVER THE CHIEF BUTLER AND THE CHIEF BAKER TO JOSEPH … FOR HE WAS NOW THE HEAD TRUSTEE OF THE PRISON

This is the point when Potiphar's day had likely changed the most. In going from the King's palace he transported these men to the prison house. Upon arriving at the prison he handed over the chief butler and the chief baker to Joseph's[10] care and oversight. (Joseph had been in the role of head trustee of the prison for some time.) Among his duties was the responsibility to document and keep the register of all the prisoners.

This encounter with Joseph would bring to mind old memories and experiences. Even though the time for Joseph to be delivered was not yet come, this encounter with him as prison administrator no doubt caused Potiphar to replay in his mind the details of so long ago.

- Was Joseph really attempting to rape his wife; or had she given him some kind of invitation to come to her bed?

- The big question was this: had she solicited Joseph to a mid-day tryst with her?

- One of the values Joseph had always displayed was good and genuine moral character. Had he misjudged Joseph's character so much before that fateful day, or had he grossly misread the situation on the day Joseph had been accused of attempted rape?

* If so, his wife had misrepresented her own part in all that had happened.

* This would mean that Joseph was innocent of all charges.

* Were things really as they appeared at the time, or had some details conveniently been left out, or altered?

As far as Potiphar was concerned, the prison warden really had it made. He remembered (possibly with regret) that when Joseph worked in his house, he was the fortunate one. Could it be that he lost Joseph's help—and for no legitimate cause? Once Potiphar's trusted servant, now he faithfully and successfully served the warden. It was possible he had misjudged the situation concerning Joseph and his wife. These were worrying thoughts.

Endnotes

1. Genesis 39:20-23 TLB
2. Genesis 39:23 KJV
3. Genesis 39:23 NIV
4. Josephus, Antiquities, Book 2, 5:1
5. Genesis 41
6. Josephus, Antiquities, Book 2, 5:1
7. Chief cupbearer: A person who serves wine, especially in a royal or noble household. In this case he is also called, "The chief butler".
8. Chief baker: A person who commands the services of baking of bread and pastries for a royal or noble household.
9. Genesis 40:1
10. Genesis 40:4

Chapter 6

THE BUTLER, THE BAKER, AND MORE DREAMS

As Joseph recorded their arrival, it was not clear just what the butler and baker had done. The king was offended. Whatever they had done was serious enough for them to have lost his favor and be remanded to this prison.

One morning, as Joseph was making his rounds to each part of the prison, he came upon the chief cupbearer and the chief baker. They were not taking their incarceration with grace and this morning seemed to be especially difficult for them. As Joseph stopped to greet them, he noticed that they were feeling low. So he asked them, "What's wrong? Why the long faces?"[1] The cupbearer responded that, besides the afflictions he underwent from the King, God did also add to him trouble from his dreams.[2]

As Joseph continued listening, both of the men said at the same time, "We both had dreams, but there is no one to interpret them."[3] Joseph said, "Don't interpretations come from God? Tell me the dreams."[4]

The chief cupbearer was the one more concerned (probably because his responsibilities had positioned him closer to Pharaoh on a regular basis) so he began telling his dream quickly. He told how in his sleep, he saw three clusters of grapes hanging upon three branches of a vine, (very) large, and ripe for gathering. He squeezed them into a cup, which the king held in his hand, and when he had strained the wine, he gave it to the king to drink, and that he received it from him with a pleasant countenance.[5]

The chief cupbearer then concluded his story by asking Joseph, "If you have any understanding in such matters, please tell me what this vision could be foretelling."[6]

Joseph smiled and spoke encouragingly to the chief cupbearer. He said, "be of good cheer, and expect to be loosed from your bonds in three days time, because the king desires your service, and is about to restore you again to it.[7] He continued, "This is what it means; the three branches are three days. Within three days Pharaoh will lift up your head and restore you to your position and you will put Pharaoh's cup into his hand, just as you used to do when you were his cupbearer."[8]

SOME LIFE CHAPTERS ARE LESS DESIRABLE THAN OTHERS—

WE TRY TO END THE UNPLEASANT ONES AS QUICKLY AS POSSIBLE, IN THE HOPE THAT THE NEXT CHAPTER WILL BE BETTER

"But when all goes well with you, remember me and show me kindness; mention me to Pharaoh and get me out of this prison. For I was forcibly carried off from the land of the Hebrews, and even here I have done nothing to deserve being put in a dungeon."[9]

There was faith in the heart of Joseph. He had a strong optimism that God, who had given to him his own dreams, would also engineer a day of deliverance.

It is difficult when we feel strongly that our day of deliverance is coming, to hold steady and allow God to deliver us on His time schedule. Our time frame is always shorter than His. Our window of opportunity is always smaller and our deadline is always closer—after all, God has no limit to His time frame and we have but seventy years to live (plus or minus).

The scripture both encourages and discourages us when it says, "… one day is with the Lord as a thousand years, and a thousand years as one day."[10]

Joseph, by asking the chief cupbearer for his assistance in obtaining a pardon, decided to help God out and move things along. However, his timing was a bit premature, because it would be two more years before the beginning of the "… seven years of great plenty."[11]

From this scene we can detect that patience is the one small character quality which Joseph struggled with for the moment. It appears that he was growing a little impatient. He could see the Lord about to deliver this pagan cupbearer, and yet he would continue to live in this dungeon.[12] In reality, Joseph was passing the test; the kind of character test we are all faced with to see if we're grasping life's lessons. Still he was a little anxious for God to quicken the pace toward his day of deliverance.

Since we do not have an accurate perspective of seeing the bigger picture, then how can we have valid insight on the best time schedule for our day of deliverance? Quite naturally we want relief from the pain, but are not always aware of the process, and the wealth of insight we gain from enduring the process.

Consider this: What would have been changed in Joseph's life if, immediately upon his return to the palace, the chief cupbearer had remembered Joseph and arranged for a royal pardon.

Picture this: Joseph, upon his release, would have been anxious to leave the big Egyptian city. Destitute and without a plan, he most certainly would have started the long and unguarded walk back to Canaan to rejoin his family.

Can you imagine these challenges?

* His dreams would have suffered failure, because he would not have been in Egypt to enter into that place of honored respect (which the dreams portrayed for him).

* His brothers still harbored hatred in their hearts for him. Their actions would have been fully exposed, because some serious debriefing would have taken place within the family forum.

* Eleven years had passed and the biggest question Jacob would have asked is: "How is it that you wound up in Egypt, anyway?"

* There would have been no apparent place for redemption, because God's plan would have been thwarted so completely.

* The years of plenty were to begin two years from the time he would have arrived in Canaan, and then, seven years later, the famine would come. Two years later they would have no Zaphnath-paaneah ruling Egypt, so going to Egypt to purchase grain would not have been an option.

* The famine, quite possibly, could have wiped out Jacob and all of his descendants.

It is good to hope for a speedy solution, but imperative to patiently wait for a divine intervention. Our destiny and life purpose are dependent on things being done God's way. Do what you can to use your creativity, but keep this in mind when looking at Joseph's story:

- The pit (dry cistern) was a safe place to imprison Joseph. This place kept Joseph in, and his murderous brothers out, so that they could all wait for the slave traders to rescue him and propel him forward to his Egypt.

- The prison was a safe place to imprison Joseph to keep him in Egypt, waiting in the wings for the day of his grand entrance into the court of Pharaoh.

- As bad as it must have been, it was the best and the safest place for him to grow and mature, meditate on his values, and continue down the road of process; a process which the Lord was using in his life to give him wisdom, insight, perspective, faith, and trust.

The chief baker sat there, stunned by what he had just heard. Another prisoner had just given divine insight into the meaning of the dream which his friend the butler had shared; and the meaning was that in three days he would be set free. Could it be, he thought, that this man, Joseph could also help me understand my dream? Almost giddy this chief baker interrupted, "In my dream there were three baskets of pastries on my head. In the top basket were all kinds of bakery goods for Pharaoh, but the birds came and ate them."[13]

"IN MY DREAM THERE WERE THREE BASKETS OF PASTRIES ON MY HEAD...BUT THE BIRDS CAME AND ATE THEM"

Joseph looked deeply into the eyes of this man and said, as he considered and reasoned about the dream, that he only wished he could be the, "… interpreter of good events to him… but he told him that he had only three days in all to live, for the three baskets signify, three days."[14] "Three days from now Pharaoh will take off your head and impale your body on a pole, and the birds will come and pick off your flesh!"[15]

Three days later it was Pharaoh's birthday and he hosted a feast for all his servants. He set the head cupbearer and the head baker in places of honor in the presence of all the guests. Then he restored the head cupbearer to his cup-bearing post; he handed Pharaoh his cup just as before. And then he impaled the head baker on a post, following Joseph's interpretations exactly. But the head cupbearer never gave Joseph another thought; he forgot all about him.[16]

Proverbs 20:21 warns us, wisely giving us a principle to live by: "An inheritance may be gotten hastily at the beginning, but the end thereof shall not be blessed."

JOSEPH WANTED A ROYAL PARDON, BUT THE PRISON WAS FOR HIS SAFETY

Joseph really wanted the chief butler to remember him and to request a royal pardon for him and a release from prison. This was not the plan of God. He had Joseph in prison for his safety and to keep him out of circulation until the right time to implement His plan.

Youth is known to be impatient. Youth has trouble understanding the blessings of time and the qualities gained in waiting. We want our inheritance early, just like the Prodigal Son,[17] but if we patiently wait for the plan which God has designed to come into being on His schedule, then we'll be more satisfied and even more gratified. Therefore, work on the ability to wait patiently.

The time had now come for Joseph to be shown as the man God had designed when He put together his destiny. He had been waiting, but so had God, and so had the elements under God's control, which were about to display a great effect upon the earth and the harvest. If there had been a *Farmers Almanac,* it would have shown the weather and harvest cycles to be in a state of altercation many years earlier. All creation was waiting for this time, and now God's man was about to be set into place and was fully prepared to give heaven's response to earth's dearth. Notice the scripture, "… all creation waits for the manifestation of the sons of God."[18]

Endnotes

1. Genesis 40:7 MSG
2. Josephus, Antiquities, Book 2, 5:1
3. Genesis 40:8 NIV
4. Genesis 40:8 MSG
5. Josephus, Antiquities, Book 2, 5:2
6. Josephus, Antiquities, Book 2, 5:2
7. Josephus, Antiquities, Book 2, 5:2
8. Genesis 40:12-13 NIV
9. Genesis 40:15 NIV
10. II Peter 3:8 KJV
11. Genesis 41:29 KJV
12. Genesis 40:15 KJV
13. Genesis 40:16-17 TLB
14. Josephus, Antiquities, Book 2, 5:3
15. Genesis 40:18-19 TLB
16. Genesis 40:20-23 MSG
17. Luke 15:11-32
18. Romans 8:19

A NEW COAT AND A NEW NAME

Joseph had been preparing for this moment without knowing any details. He lay on his mat in the prison, while Pharaoh lay in his soft bed in the Palace.

Joseph's night was peaceful and restful. Pharaoh, though he could not understand why, or how, or when, was about to begin a new chapter. His night visions so unsettled him that Pharaoh was like batter in a bowl, when the big wooden spoon is set to stir. He awakened suddenly while Joseph slept soundly.

God was speaking to this world leader, but he knew not the voice of God; so he was stirred by a strange concern.

Two full years had passed since Joseph had interpreted the night visions of the chief cupbearer and the chief baker. Though Joseph had asked to be remembered to Pharaoh, the chief cupbearer had forgotten. Now Pharaoh was being moved from sleep, because God determined that, "Now is the time."[1]

In the darkest of the night Pharaoh was awakened by two separate night visions. He was troubled in his spirit.

Morning finally came. Pharaoh called together the wisest men among the Egyptians, desiring to learn from them the interpretation of his dreams. But when they hesitated and could not give the meaning, the King became even more disturbed. It was at this time that the King's cupbearer remembered all that he had forgotten from two years past. He saw the confusion that Pharaoh was in, and realized that now was the time to share with him about the Hebrew slave.[2]

TIMING IS VERY IMPORTANT... THE BUTLER HAD FAILED, BUT NOW WAS THE PERFECT TIME

Timing is very important. The cupbearer was frustrated because he'd failed to remember Joseph to Pharaoh, but it is evident that now was the perfect time.

Joseph had vague ideas of God's plan for his life. He was aware of the daily details, but could not bring the big picture clearly into focus. As a result, he had to depend on the time factor to just play itself out. There was no specific course of action he could take to accelerate God's plan. We also face times when we have to relax and just keep on living, making ourselves available, thus allowing God to continue putting the pieces of life's puzzle together on His schedule.

The wine tasting, chief cupbearer (butler) was a man who had sincerely meant to speak of Joseph to Pharaoh when he was first released from prison, but God withheld Joseph from memory until the timing was right. Then, in an unsuspecting moment the still small voice[3] prompted this cupbearer to speak to Pharaoh about Joseph.[4]

The timing was perfect. God had prepared Pharaoh during the night with dreams—now Joseph's destiny will unfold before him.

It would have been a mistake for the cupbearer to remember Joseph's abilities before now. However, now was the time to step up to the line, spare no details, and tell Pharaoh all he knew about the Hebrew in the prison of Potiphar.

The cupbearer fully disclosed his story to Pharaoh. "I just now remembered something—I'm sorry, I should have told you this long ago. Once when Pharaoh got angry with his servants, he locked me, and the head baker in the house of the captain of the guard. We both had dreams on the same night, each dream with its own meaning. It so happened that there was a young Hebrew slave there with us; he belonged to Potiphar, the captain of the guard. We told him our dreams and he interpreted them for us, each dream separately. Things turned out just as he interpreted. I was returned to my position and the head baker was impaled."[5]

The cupbearer continued, "If you will send for him, and not despise him for his misfortune of being in prison, then you will learn what your dreams signify."[6]

Pharaoh was glad for the report by the cupbearer and sent at once for Joseph. He was brought hastily from the dungeon, and after a quick shave and change of clothes, came in before Pharaoh.[7]

The people who lived in Canaan (as well as many other Eastern nations) found it distasteful, culturally, to shave. As a result, all the men had mature beards. However, in Egypt, all of the men detested long beards, and adhered to a strict custom of shaving daily.[8] It is interesting to realize that the Hebrews would only shave as a sign of mourning; the Egyptians would only let their beards grow when mourning. In prison Joseph had let his hair grow, but now shaved in accordance with custom.[9]

Joseph arrived, being escorted by servants. Pharaoh said to Joseph, as he welcomed him into his court, "… my servant bears witness that you are at present the best and most skillful person I can consult with."[10]

"I HAD A DREAM LAST NIGHT … AND NONE OF THESE MEN CAN TELL ME WHAT IT MEANS"

"I had a dream last night … and none of these men can tell me what it means."[11] "But I've heard that just by hearing a dream you can interpret it. That is why I have called for you."[12]

"I cannot do it," Joseph replied to Pharaoh, "but God will give Pharaoh the answer he desires."[13]

Pharaoh said, "I was standing upon the bank of the Nile River, when suddenly, seven fat, healthy-looking cows came up out of the river and began grazing along the river bank. But then seven other cows came up from the river, very skinny and bony—in fact, I've never seen such poor-looking specimens in all the land of Egypt. And these skinny cattle ate up the seven fat ones that had come out first, and afterwards they were still as skinny as before! Then I woke up."[14]

Pharaoh continued his story. He immediately launched into telling about the second dream: "I saw seven ears of corn growing out of one root, having their heads born down by the weight of the grains, and bending down with the fruit, which was now ripe and fit for reaping; and near these I saw seven other ears of corn, meager and weak, for want of rain."[15] "… and scorched by the east wind."[16] "And the thin ears swallowed up the full ears. I've told all this to my magicians, but not one of them could tell me the meaning."[17]

"Then Joseph said to Pharaoh, 'The dreams of Pharaoh are one and the same. God has revealed to Pharaoh what He is about to do. The seven good cows are seven years, and the seven good heads of corn are seven years; it is one and the same dream. The seven lean, ugly cows that came up afterwards are seven years, and so are the seven worthless heads of corn scorched by the east wind: They are seven years of famine.'[18] 'So God has showed you what He is about to do: The next seven years will be a period of great prosperity throughout all the land of Egypt; but afterwards there will be seven years of famine so great that all the prosperity will be forgotten and wiped out; famine will consume the land. The famine will be so terrible that even the memory of the good years will be erased. The double dream gives double impact, showing that what I have told you is certainly going to happen, for God has decreed it, and it is going to happen soon.'"[19]

Pharaoh listened attentively to all that Joseph had said and was in wonder at the discretion and wisdom of Joseph. Pharaoh then began to speak, asking Joseph to indicate to him how he would advise him to carry out the preparation necessary during the years of plenty, so that they would be prepared during the great famine, which was to come.[20]

Joseph gave this wisdom to Pharaoh, "My suggestion is that you find the wisest man in Egypt and put him in charge of administering a nation-wide farm program. Let Pharaoh divide Egypt into five administrative districts, and let the officials of these districts gather into the royal storehouses all the excess crops of the next seven years, so that there will be enough to eat when the seven years of famine come. Otherwise, disaster will surely strike."[21]

Joseph continued by giving counsel that Pharaoh not permit the people to lavish upon themselves the luxury of excess, but to reserve the extra for the future, when prosperity may not be so

JOSEPH WAS ESPECIALLY ENDOWED WITH INSIGHT INTO THE REALM OF DREAMS

great. He further advised that care be taken to allow the husbandmen only what would be sufficient for feeding them and their families. Pharaoh was intrigued at how Joseph had such insight that he could both accurately interpret dreams, and issue forth, what seemed to be a higher level of natural wisdom in his counsel. He had never seen such wisdom come from any one of those who were among his seers. This Hebrew proved to be quite amazing to Pharaoh. He could see that Joseph was especially endowed with an intuitive insight into the realm of dreams; but he was further amazed as he realized that his own greatest need was in the area of wisdom.[22] Every leader must have trusted counselors gathered around him to impart new ideas so that his own world-view can be expanded.

Joseph was a wise and perceptive man. He had the spiritual awareness to search deep within his heart, and to listen intently to the voice of God, which would give him the guidance he needed when faced with tough questions. Like Daniel,[23] Joseph was kept current with whatever the challenge of any outside force by the fact that the spirit of God dwelt within him.[24] He possessed a special understanding when he was asked to interpret dreams and hard questions. Joseph had learned to live in the shadow of the Almighty[25] and how to sit down in … God's presence.[26] As a result he could draw on the divine wisdom of the Lord, thus enabling him to dissolve doubt, interpret dreams,[27] and even to understand the times.[28] Joseph's word of knowledge[29] was perfect for the challenge Pharaoh presented.

Whenever a believer faces a problem, it is a must to dip deep down into the well of the Holy Spirit for a God-given Word of Wisdom[30] for the moment. It happened in the Old Testament with many like Solomon,[31] and also with Joseph as he gave additional counsel to Pharaoh after interpreting the dreams.[32]

The mood in that great hall of Pharaoh's court moved from anxious concern to hope and calm. Because of the wisdom which came so naturally from him when he spoke, Joseph was one who could set his listeners at ease.

Joseph was a good man to converse with on any level, but when he was faced with interpreting dreams there was a special anointing. This was Joseph's realm and no one did it better than him; because the dreams he addressed were always of Divine origin and were far-reaching in their impact. For these challenges, Joseph was surely and fully equipped.

An amazing peace settled over the court of Pharaoh as Joseph moved from invited guest to man in control. The scripture says, "When the righteous are in authority, the people rejoice; but when a wicked man rules, the people groan."[33]

In Pharaoh's court, on that day, it was somewhat like what took place on that ship in the Mediterranean Sea with the Apostle Paul on board. The people on board the ship were given assurance and comfort when Paul spoke of the visit of the Angel to encourage them that all would be saved, but the ship would be lost.[34]

It was the same kind of hope and calmness which now settled over Pharaoh and all those present before Joseph.

Also present in the court was the counsel of wise men and officials who daily advised Pharaoh. Everyone had a vested interest in knowing how Pharaoh would respond when dealing with such matters. Pharaoh had called for all the magicians of Egypt and all its wise men ... Pharaoh told them his dreams, but there was no one who could interpret them.[35] Egyptians had a strong respect for mysticism, superstition, and magic. The magicians and wise men had been as dumbfounded as Pharaoh and this young Hebrew man, Joseph, had given them answers to their questions and resolution to their fears. The mood of this body of leaders had little doubt as to what was about to happen, for a consensus of respect was forming in their thoughts that this man, Joseph, was a rare man of exceptional insight and leadership

It was customary for Potiphar, the captain of Pharaoh's bodyguard, to be present to witness the proceedings which took place in Pharaoh's court. One of the primary reasons for his required presence had to do with his being witness to any offence, which might be committed against Pharaoh;[36] while another being the logic that he was a member of the personal counsel of Pharaoh and would be required to give his voice to affirm that wise counsel was being followed.

On the day when Joseph stood before Pharaoh to interpret his dreams, Potiphar must have seen his opportunity to question Pharaoh's appraisal that Joseph was, discreet and wise.[37] After all it was in the arena of discretion that Joseph had been accused (by Potiphar's wife) and was imprisoned.

TIME OFTEN HEALS—SURELY TIME REVEALS THE OTHER SIDE OF THE STORY

Time often heals—surely time reveals the other side of the story. This may have been the case in this one.

64

It is very likely that Potiphar's wife's immoral character has been revealed during the years since she attempted to tempt Joseph with her enticements.[38] This may be the reason Potiphar gave no comments on the day Joseph was promoted over all the land.

The court of Pharaoh was motionless for a moment as everyone from Pharaoh to his advisors and servants took in all that Joseph had said. A plan was forming in the mind of Pharaoh and the favor of God was building in the hearts of all those present.

Pharaoh began to speak to Joseph of his respect for the great words of wisdom, which he had spoken. They had been awed by what the dreams had really meant, and were now prepared to respond just as Joseph had advised. So much was at stake. Serious consideration must be given to what had been predicted. Pharaoh considered his own wisdom and decided that, "he who first discovers significant solutions just may be the best overseer of it."[39]

Looking around the large hall, Pharaoh began to speak what everyone was thinking, "Can we find anyone like this man, one in whom is the spirit of God?"[40] "Who could do it better than Joseph? He is a man who is obviously filled with the Spirit of God." As Pharaoh turned toward Joseph he said, "Since God has revealed the meaning of the dreams to you, you are the wisest man in the country! I am hereby appointing you to be in charge. What you say goes, throughout all the land of Egypt."[41] "You shall be over my house, and all my people shall be ruled according to your word;"[42] "Only with respect to the throne will I be greater than you."[43]

Pharaoh said to Joseph, "I hereby put you in charge of the whole land of Egypt." Then Pharaoh took his signet ring from his finger and put it on Joseph's finger. He dressed him in robes of fine linen and put a gold chain around his neck.[44] He then ordered that Joseph should ride in the second chariot, and they must cry out before him, "Bow the knee!"[45] Pharaoh made a pledge to Joseph, "I am Pharaoh and without your consent no man may lift his hand or foot in all the land of Egypt."[46]

Pharaoh gave to Joseph significant gifts

He gave Joseph his signet ring. Engraved upon this ring was an Egyptian cartouche[47] with Pharaoh's name in hieroglyphics. This was a custom, which was thought to protect the one whose name was engraved within the borders of the design. The seal was also the king's signature, thus giving Joseph the power of attorney to transact business in the king's name.

Pharaoh took off his ring from his hand, and put it upon Joseph's hand.[48] This symbolized a covenant of friendship and trust, which automatically raised Joseph to a higher level than any other of Pharaoh' trusted advisers. On that day, Joseph stepped through a door, which would mean greater freedom and autonomy than he had ever dreamed possible. The ring said volumes to every Egyptian who ever observed it upon his finger. This meant more than just being an administrator, as he had been for Potiphar. This symbolized a covenant, which meant that he was the friend of Pharaoh. It was a clear indication that Joseph was assuming, to a large extent, the identity of Pharaoh and his family. This act by Pharaoh (in embracing Joseph) must not be under-valued if we are to appreciate the role and responsibility he is to occupy in the continuing story.

> JOSEPH WAS ASSUMING, TO A LARGE EXTENT, THE IDENTITY OF PHARAOH AND HIS FAMILY

He arrayed him in vestures of fine linen.[49] This was a step further in the covenant which involved the ring. None of the advisers to Pharaoh had been afforded such royal treatment. None of them wore a ring granting such a high level of authority, and none of them were elevated to wearing robes made of linen or silk, which was generally worn only by the Egyptian priesthood (to which the king, himself belonged).[50]

He placed a gold chain around his neck. Pharaoh fully dressed Joseph on that day in the great court of Egypt. If anyone were to miss the ring, they certainly would see the gold chain about his neck. This chain was a symbol of dignity and honor worn by all rulers and people of high rank.[51]

Joseph was to ride in the second chariot. Pharaoh made a declaration, as he had begun this ceremony. "Since God has made all this known to you, there is no one so discerning and wise as you. You shall be in charge of my palace, and all my people are to submit to your orders. Only with respect to the throne will I be greater than you."[52] He then invited Joseph to take possession of and ride in the second chariot. He was not invited to ride in the second chariot as a guest would do, but, in effect, was saying, "This will be your mode of transportation, as the number two man in the land." This was another way of saying "only in regard to the throne will I be greater than you."[53] Pharaoh gave the command on that day—as Joseph was to ride down any of Egypt's streets, the command would be issued ahead of him, "Bow the knee,"[54] and the people would give him honor as they bowed.

Pharaoh gave to Joseph a wife. Another gift given to Joseph was a wife. The girl was the daughter of the prominent priest of the city of On. Her name was Asenath, and her father's name was Potipherah.[55]

Pharaoh decided that Joseph should be given a new name. Pharaoh considered Joseph's name and determined that things would work better if he were called by an Egyptian name rather than to retain a Hebrew, or foreign name. So he designated that Joseph would be called, Zaphnath-paaneah. After all, it would be better to have an Egyptian in a high position of authority in the land.

Joseph's name was Hebrew and meant, *"God shall add."* Upon coming to Egypt and, in due course of time, we see that Joseph was given a new alias, which is common practice when looking back over history. Even in the twenty-first century, when an individual moves from one culture to another (particularly when the culture or language to which they come is extremely different from their own) it is customary practice to christen them with a new and more local name or nickname.

The new name was probably given in this case to hide the fact that this honored Egyptian official was actually a foreigner. There would be no reason to explain, for example, that the man over all the agricultural and food industry was in fact a Hebrew who came up through the ranks of slavery and the prison system.

> ZAPHNATH-PAANEAH WAS NOT AN EGYPTIAN, BUT A FOREIGNER

The name Zaphnath-paaneah had several facets and meanings to it. When it came across the hearing of the Egyptians, this name meant:

- *"The revealer of secrets"*[56]
- *"Abundance of life"*[57]
- *"Savior of the world"*[58]
- *"God speaks and He lives."*[59]

Did Pharaoh make it known to the Egyptian people that there was going to be a fourteen year period where they would be first blessed with abnormal prosperity, and then cursed by prolonged famine? Did he announce to the public that they were about to go through seven years of great plenty followed by seven years of famine? The answer is found in the writings of Flavius Josephus: "But Joseph having this power given him by the king, with leave to make use of his seal, and to wear purple, drove in his chariot through all the land of Egypt, and took the corn of the husbandmen, allotting as much to everyone as would be sufficient for seed and for food, but without discovering to anyone the reason why he did so."[60]

This last phrase "… without discovering to anyone the reason why he did so," shows that, in fact, only those in Pharaoh's inner circle of government had any knowledge of the events surrounding Pharaoh's dreams, Joseph's interpreting of those dreams, his imprisonment, or his unique rise to power. If the general public had known, it is likely that there would have been panic and fear in the hearts of the people.

Therefore, wisdom dictated secrecy and stern discipline to manage the harvests. This secrecy insured that when the years of scarcity came, suffering would not be felt by the Egyptians.[61]

Endnotes

1. Ecclesiastes 3:1-8
2. Josephus, Antiquities, Book 2, 5:4
3. I Kings 19:12 KJV
4. Genesis 41:9-13
5. Genesis 41:9-13 MSG
6. Josephus, Antiquities, Book 2, 5:4
7. Genesis 41:14 TLB
8. "It is worthy of note that when we visited Egypt, the guides told us that the beards seen on the tall statues of the Pharaohs do not imply that Pharaoh's grew beards, but are only fake beards put on the statues to signify wisdom." Ron A. Bishop
9. Dake's Bible, page 40, "O"
10. Josephus, Antiquities, Book 2, 5:5
11. Genesis 41:15 TLB
12. Genesis 41:15 MSG
13. Genesis 41:16 NIV
14. Genesis 41:17-21 TLB
15. Josephus, Antiquities, Book 2, 5:5
16. Genesis 41:23 NIV
17. Genesis 41:24 TLB
18. Genesis 41:25-27 NIV
19. Genesis 41:28-32 TLB
20. Josephus, Antiquities, Book 2, 5:7
21. Genesis 41:33-36 TLB
22. Josephus, Antiquities, Book 2, 5:7
23. Daniel 5:10-12
24. Daniel 5:11; Genesis 41:38
25. Psalm 91:1 TLB
26. Psalm 91:1 MSG
27. Daniel 5:12
28. I Chronicles 12:32
29. I Chronicles 12:8
30. I Corinthians 12:8
31. I Kings 3:16-28
32. Genesis 41:33-36
33. Proverbs 29:2 NKJV
34. Acts 27:21-26
35. Genesis 41:8 NKJV
36. Genesis 40:1-3
37. Genesis 41:39 KJV
38. Genesis 39:7
39. Josephus, Antiquities, Book 2, 5:7

40. Genesis 41:37 NIV
41. Genesis 41:39-40 TLB
42. Genesis 41:40 NKJV
43. Genesis 41:40 NIV
44. Genesis 41:41-42 NIV
45. Genesis 41:43 NKJV
46. Genesis 41:44 NKJV
47. "An oval or oblong design, especially on an Egyptian monument, bearing the title of a king." New Webster's Dictionary and Thesaurus of the English Language. Lexicon Publications, Inc., Danbury, CT. Copyright 1972, Page 151
48. Genesis 41:42
49. Genesis 41:42 KJV
50. Dake's Bible, Page 41, "F"
51. Dake's Bible, Page 41, "G"
52. Genesis 41:39-40 NIV
53. Genesis 41:40 NKJV
54. Genesis 41:43 KJV
55. Genesis 41:45
56. Josephus, Antiquities, Book 2, 6:1
57. Dake's Bible, page 41, "J"
58. Taken from the writings of Saint Jerome (c.347-September 30, 420)
59. Genesis 41:44 MSG
60. Josephus, Antiquities, Book 2, 5:7
61. Josephus, Antiquities, Book 2, 5:6

The Joseph Story

Chapter 8

ZAPHNATH-PAANEAH MAKES HIS MARK

Joseph was thirty years of age when these changes came into his life. He wasted no time in assuming the responsibility of his new role. Immediately, Joseph began touring the entire land of Egypt to evaluate the scope of potential harvest, and establishing himself into the role as administrator.[1]

In the seven abundant years the earth brought forth by handfuls, for each seed planted.[2] Joseph requisitioned for the government a portion of all the crops grown throughout Egypt.[3] "In each city he put the food grown in the fields surrounding it. Joseph stored up huge quantities of corn, like the sand of the sea; it was so much that he stopped keeping records, because it was beyond measure."[4]

God has Helped me Forget the Past

At this point in Joseph's life, the blessings of God began to fall upon him. He became aware that God was determined to bring to him personal benefits and fruitfulness. He and Asenath had been enjoying their new life together, and now was the time that God would show them His pleasure. The firstborn son of Joseph and Asenath brought great joy to their home.

Joseph put much thought into the name he would give to his firstborn as the lifelong mark to identify his son apart from all others. These days were different for Joseph, as they were filled with peace instead of conflict. Now their new son would help to make all his hopes and dreams become a reality. He felt whole; he felt complete. Life had become good for this son of Jacob.

He had memories of Jacob and his family, but they were fading and seemed so distant. Crowding out the difficult memories of so long ago were Joseph's new home, his lovely wife, and especially now his newborn son. Yes, he longed to see his father and his younger brother, Benjamin. With wisdom, he left these loved ones in the hands of God, trusting Him to bring them back into his life if it should be His will and plan. Finally, he had made his decision. His name shall be Manasseh. Why Manasseh? In Hebrew the name Manasseh means, *"forgetting the past."*

> HIS NAME SHALL
> BE MANASSEH,
> TO HELP FORGET
> THE PAST

As for now, it felt good for Joseph to leave off his Hebrew heritage and apply himself to his new post here in Egypt. He was Zaphnath-paaneah, and life had so many new requirements. He must use his strength, his energy, and his best skills to prepare this great land for the challenging times which soon lay ahead. His new son, Manasseh, would be a blessing to help him focus on the things at hand and forget the irreparable things of the past. There had been nights when he had awakened from a deep sleep to remember, all too well, the anguish he had felt when he had entered his brothers' camp in the desert of Dothan, only to be beaten and cast into the pit, to await being sold into slavery to strangers. Manasseh would be his reminder that all those dark memories would be replaced with happy ones. Joseph realized that his Hebrew heart would be strengthened every time he called his son's name.

I Now Live a Fruitful Life

All of Egypt was well into the seven years of plenty and great prosperity. Joseph enjoyed his life and especially his family. It had been some time since he had put much thought to Canaan and all that it conjured up in his mind. These days were happy and fun for him. There was lots of work, but he always made sure he left time for Asenath and Manasseh.

Now that his second son had just been born, he began to review his progress and meditate about exactly where he was in life. When it came time to give this child a name Joseph mused over all the favor and blessings, which had come his way.

Joseph thought about why he had given Manasseh such a name—one which reflected how God had helped him forget the toil and all that was negatively attached to his youth. He considered now the progress he had made and the prosperity he had enjoyed.

He settled on the name, Ephraim. Joseph thought, "God has made me fruitful in this land of my slavery."[5]

The Egyptians enjoyed the first seven years of Joseph's reign as Prime Minister. The people of the land felt secure, and had no knowledge of what lay just ahead, but Pharaoh was fully expecting this famine because of Joseph's insight.[6] "Now after Egypt had happily passed over seven years... the famine came upon them in the eighth year."[7]

Because the people of Egypt were not expecting it, they were especially distraught at being inconvenienced and afflicted when the first harvest failed. They came running to the king's gates, begging for help.[8]

Endnotes

1. Genesis 41:46
2. Genesis 41:47 AMP
3. Genesis 41:48 TLB
4. Genesis 41:48, 49 NIV
5. Genesis 41:52 TLB
6. Josephus, Antiquities, Book 2, 5:7
7. Josephus, Antiquities, Book 2, 6:1
8. Josephus, Antiquities, Book 2, 6:1

Chapter 9

BAD NEWS—
GOOD OUTCOME

Pharaoh felt smug and elated. He could see clearly that he had made the right decision in his appointment of Joseph. If there had ever been a doubt, there was not one now—the famine had come precisely when Joseph had prophesied.

Because of Joseph, Pharaoh was Relevant

Egypt was on the inside track. They were on the cutting edge. Their future looked secure—all because they had Joseph as their Prime Minister and chief ruler of the land. The years of prosperity had been described as happy years.[1] The years of famine could at least be tolerable, because of Joseph's administration during the times of plenty. Although there was scarcity,[2] there was also confidence that they had done all that was necessary. They were fully prepared for whatever the years would hurl their way. Now they had only to ride out these seven years with Joseph at the helm.

An appropriate scripture for Joseph's rule is this: "When the [uncompromisingly] righteous are in authority, the people rejoice; but when the wicked man rules, the people groan and sigh."[3] The harvest had been abundant, but now there were crop failures in Egypt and "in all the surrounding countries too, but in Egypt there was plenty of grain in the storehouses. The people began to starve. They pleaded with Pharaoh for food."[4] Then Pharaoh told all the Egyptians, "Go to Zaphnath-paaneah and do what he tells you."[5]

PROSPERITY YIELDED TO FAMINE

Joseph knew exactly what to expect when the prosperous times yielded to famine. He had set up distribution centers well in advance and had given strict training on all that must be done to survive when the crops would fail. The great Zaphnath-paaneah was not taken by surprise when the agricultural economy totally collapsed. He and all those under his employ, as well as Pharaoh himself, were fully prepared and waiting.

Not only were they fully prepared to feed all the Egyptians, but they had also made policies favorable to selling food to the other nations who would be in the same famine. Joseph never forgot his own roots. He knew this famine would reach farther than the borders of Egypt. He realized he must be a wise steward of the harvests which had been entrusted to his care. Therefore, he had been careful to set policies so that strangers had liberty to buy also. He recognized that he must make the benefits of the Egyptians also available to their neighbors. He must share the happiness with those who were in misfortune.[6]

Egyptian Economics

The Egyptian economy climbed to high levels during the years of prosperity. Then, when famine struck the land, the economy soared even higher.

Regional economies go high or low based, in part, on the availability of food supplies as well as the level of preparedness of those who lead during times of natural disasters.

While other neighboring nations struggled with the dearth of the present famine, Egypt saw their treasury rising with the sale of every bag of grain.

This wise Egyptian ruler, Zaphnath-paaneah, had stored up all the excess grains during the prosperous years rather than permit the Egyptians to eat or sell them luxuriously. He gave strong leadership and required that the people of the land must, "… reserve what they would have spent in luxury beyond their necessity, against the time of want."[7]

Pharaoh saw the circumstances that had developed around Joseph and the first years of his leadership as being invigorating. His own popularity was at an all time high as a result of Joseph.

Egypt was also popular with the other nations around them because, when the continent was hungry, the Egyptians were full and had surplus. Not only this, but their ruler (Zaphnath-paaneah) was generous and welcomed other peoples to freely come and buy whatever they needed. This brought favor and good will to Egypt in the international arena.

Back in the land of Canaan, Jacob (or Israel[8] as he had been called), was a wise old Patriarch and was always aware of what was going on around him. He learned that the famine reached far beyond his local area, throughout Canaan and even into Egypt. Egypt, however, was better prepared than anyone else and actually had put the news out that there was grain available. When he learned that foreigners were welcomed to come and buy, Jacob sent all his sons into Egypt to buy corn.[9] Before his ten older sons left Hebron, Jacob said to them, "Go down and buy some for us before we all starve to death."[10]

Why All of Jacob's Sons?

In this story it is interesting that *all* the sons of Jacob chose to go to Egypt, rather than just a smaller group of them. It would seem more likely that they should have left some sons behind to protect the family in their absence. Notice that Jacob had a small army in his employ, as had his grandfather, Abraham.[11] It appears that security was not a major concern. As it happened, all the older male sons of Jacob went to Egypt.

These ten sons left Jacob and all their families and servants behind to go to a land they had never seen before. Only Benjamin remained behind. He was not permitted to accompany them, partly because he was the only remaining son of Rachel,[12] and also for fear some harm might happen to him, as it had to his brother Joseph.

TEN OF JACOB'S SONS TRAVEL TO EGYPT TO BUY GRAIN

Egypt had made volumes of grain available based on the quota or ration system. Perhaps Jacob thought that more grain could be acquired if more delegates were present. He (no doubt) felt that the more men he sent, the more grain he could purchase. If he sent a smaller delegation, perhaps they could not secure enough grain to sustain all of those who were dependant upon him. So it was that Jacob's sons traveled to Egypt along with many others from many lands to buy food.

No Clue

Joseph was the governor over all the land of Egypt and responsible for the distribution centers in every one of the five administrative districts.[13] However, he was personally responsible for the central district, where all foreigners were required to apply for the right to make purchases. When Joseph's ten brothers arrived in Egypt they, quite naturally, found their way into the court of the Egyptian Governor Zaphnath-paaneah.

They had no clue that this great Egyptian governor could be their brother Joseph; and bowed low before him, with their faces to the earth.

Endnotes

1. Josephus, Antiquities, Book 2, 5:7
2. Josephus, Antiquities, Book 2, 5:6
3. Proverbs 29:2 AMP
4. Genesis 41:55 TLB
5. Genesis 41:55 NIV
6. Josephus, Antiquities, Book 2, 6:1
7. Josephus, Antiquities, Book 2, 5:7
8. Genesis 42:1-2
9. Josephus, Antiquities, Book 2, 6:2
10. Genesis 42:2 TLB
11. Genesis 14:12-16
12. Josephus, Antiquities, Book 2, 6:2
13. Genesis 41:35 TLB

Chapter 10

THE TEST OF CHARACTER

Joseph was Unrecognizable to his Brothers

Joseph was seventeen years old when he was sold into slavery.[1] He became governor over Egypt when he was thirty.[2] The seven years of prosperity brought him to age thirty-seven. At the second year of the famine, when Joseph was thirty-nine, his brothers came to purchase grain from him.[3]

Joseph had been in Egypt for twenty-two years, whereas he had only lived in Canaan for seventeen years. The years had changed him. His clothing was significantly different; his hair was cut differently and he had no beard at all (although he may have had little beard when he was age seventeen). It is not unreasonable that the brothers did not recognize Joseph. Keep in mind that none of these brothers had seen each other clean-shaven since their youth. The question remains if they would have recognized each other quickly had they been under similar circumstances. Also consider that they did not hear Joseph speak Hebrew (his native tongue), but only Arabic, the language of Egypt.

Add to this the quiet voice of Joseph and the bold voice of an interpreter (who must impress the great Zaphnath-paaneah with his skill) and you have ten insecure foreign men who are afraid for the outcome.

JOSEPH WAS QUIET

HIS INTERPRETER WAS LOUD

AND THE HEBREW BROTHERS WERE INSECURE

Joseph recognized these men immediately as his brothers, but decided he must take care to know what was in their hearts before he should reveal his true identity. He called for an interpreter to assist him in communicating with these Hebrews.[4] There was no chance that they identified him, because he was very young when he left them. He was now so much older and had experienced a great deal—the lines of his face were changed, making him almost unrecognizable. Add to that the absolute greatness of his regal dignity as a formidable ruler and it is out of the question that anyone had any suspicion, whatsoever.[5]

"Where have you come from?" Joseph quizzed through the tongue of the interpreter.

"From Canaan … we've come to buy food."[6]

As Joseph observed their countenance and thought back over those years, he also remembered the dreams he had dreamed of them.[7] Joseph refused to sell them corn and accused them. He charged that they had come as spies of the king's affairs, and that they came from several countries. He insisted that they had joined themselves together, and pretended that they were all from one family. He added that it was just not possible that a private man should breed so many sons.[8]

One of the reasons Joseph was so demanding of his brothers was that he wanted to push them far enough that they would volunteer more details as to the wellbeing of their father, Jacob, especially as to his current state. He was not content just to find out their attitude toward him, but also to gain information as to whether or not his father was still alive. He was driven by his own curiosity of how his father had taken his disappearance, and finally to discover if Benjamin had survived as well. One thing that was disturbing him deeply was the concern that his brothers may have ventured down the same path (in their disdain for the sons of Rachel) and had done to Benjamin what they had done to him.[9]

They defended themselves saying, "Sir, there are twelve of us brothers, and our father is in the land of Canaan. Our youngest brother is there with our father, and one of our brothers is dead."[10]

It is evident that Joseph is in charge of this visit. He has successfully led them down the road of distraction and terror, causing them to fear for their own safety. They feared that very great danger hung over them.

THEY HAD TOLD THIS LIE SO MANY TIMES THEY BELIEVED IT THEMSELVES

It is interesting that these brothers of Joseph had deceived themselves by rehearsing the lie that Joseph was dead by now. They had no other answer. They could have been more accurate by saying, "We sold him into slavery and now have no idea where he is." They might have at least answered, "Our brother Joseph is lost and we do not know where to find him."

Instead they elected to make the default statement: "Our brother is dead."[11] They were not aware, but they certainly told the wrong man that Joseph had died. Zaphnath-paaneah had shaved Joseph's beard just that morning—he could personally verify that he was very much alive!

Joseph was well-hidden behind the alias identity of Zaphnath-paaneah, and it worked well for him. The anonymity allowed him to discover exactly what had taken place with his father and with Benjamin after he had moved on to Egypt.

Reuben had assumed the role of spokesman and pleaded their defense before this court.[12] Joseph's brothers were deeply concerned about their own welfare. They were distracted and had no idea of the connection between Joseph and Zaphnath-paaneah. Reuben continued his defense saying that they had not come to Egypt with any ill intention. They had no desire to bring any harm to the king's affairs.[13] He invited Joseph to look at them, to see the family resemblance, even to the lines in their faces. He pleaded his case that they all had the same common blood, and asked Joseph to look closely at them and see that they did not look so different from one another.

Reuben said, "Our father's name is Jacob, an Hebrew man, who had twelve of us for his sons by four wives; which twelve of us, while we were all alive, were a happy family; but when one of our brethren, whose name was Joseph, died, our affairs changed for the worse; for our father could not forbear to make a long lamentation for him; and we are in affliction, both by the calamity of the death of our brother, and the miserable state of our aged father."[14]

Joseph's brothers, when selling Joseph, had not taken into account just how great the loss would be to their father. Certainly they never considered how great a suffering they would inflict upon themselves. Their actions proved to be some of the arrows which were shot against Joseph. They would find that the arrows they shot at him would even come back to pierce them.[15]

It was good for Joseph to find out that both Benjamin and their father, Jacob, were alive and well in Canaan.

Joseph said to them, "Even if you say that you have a younger brother and that he is with your father, how am I to know you are telling the truth? I say you are spies."[16]

As Joseph was considering his next step, he felt strongly that he must find out their moral character and the motives of their hearts. He decided that he should buy a little time by putting them all in prison for a few days before sending any of them away to Canaan.

THE EGYPTIAN RULER HELD THE HEBREWS IN PRISON TO GET THEIR FULL ATTENTION ... A FULL THREE DAYS

"This is the way I will test your story: I swear by the life of Pharaoh that you are not going to leave Egypt until this youngest brother comes here. One of you must go and get your brother! I'll keep the rest of you here, bound in prison. Then we'll find out whether your story is true or not. If it turns out that you don't have a younger brother, then I'll know you are spies."

So he gave instruction that they be taken from his court and held in prison. They remained in prison for three days. Joseph ordered that they be brought to stand before him. These were his remarks on that day: "I am a God-fearing man and I'm going to give you an opportunity to prove yourselves. I'm going to take a chance that you are honorable; only one of you shall remain in chains in jail, and the rest of you may go on home with grain for your families; but bring your youngest brother back to me. In this way I will know whether you are telling me the truth; and if you are, I will spare you." To this they agreed.[17]

The Dark Secret in their Family Closet

"I told you so. You should have listened to me."

While still standing in Joseph's court these brothers gathered together and began to debrief on what had just happened. "Speaking among themselves, they said, 'This has all happened because of what we did to Joseph long ago. We saw his terror and anguish and heard his pleadings, but we wouldn't listen.'"

This was likely the first time in years these brothers had had an open discussion of the events surrounding Joseph's ill treatment at their hands twenty-two years earlier. It had been a subject which they had all avoided very carefully, lest they open themselves to exposure and the judgment of their father. Reuben was grieved at his brothers for what they had done to Joseph, and used this occasion to tell them so. He spoke most directly to his brothers accusing them of being a bit late in their repentance. He admonished them to bear whatever comes with patience, because now they would be powerless to control

THOUGH THE BROTHERS WERE NOT AWARE, JOSEPH UNDERSTOOD EVERY WORD THEY SAID

88

the outcome. They all agreed that this calamity had been brought upon them as punishment by God.[18]

Reuben said, "Didn't I tell you not to do it? But you wouldn't listen. And now we're going to die because we murdered him. Of course they didn't know that Joseph understood their words, as he was standing there, for he had been speaking to them through an interpreter! Now he left the room and found a place where he could weep.

Shout it From the Housetops

We can depend on the certainty of God's principle that, "Nothing is so closely covered up that it will not be revealed, or hidden that it will not be known. Whatever you have spoken in the darkness shall be heard and listened to in the light, and what you have whispered in people's ears and behind closed doors will be proclaimed upon the housetops."[19]

These brothers were in a genuine dilemma. They had covered up their sin, and it was about to be revealed. Often men do things which they hope will be left covered until after their death, but seldom does it take the Holy Spirit that long. The reason it will surely be revealed is that the Lord really does want to redeem us. The only way this redemptive process can take place is if the sin is uncovered. This is the grace of God that is out to expose evil ways and evil deeds. Yes, it is harder on the flesh in the short term, but it is better for our spirit and our eternity if redemption takes place before the grave.

Upon returning to the court, Joseph selected Simeon, the second oldest brother, from among them and had him bound before their eyes.[20]

Why did Joseph Choose Simeon?

It is purely speculation when responding to the question of why Joseph selected Simeon to actually remain behind in the prison of Egypt.[21]

- It may have been a purely random pick.

- It could have been the murderous look in Simeon's eyes on the day when Joseph was removed from his donkey and cast into the pit.

- It is likely that, even after so many years, Joseph suspected that there were issues in Simeon's life which were never resolved. It is reasonable to believe that of the two offenders in the story of Genesis 34, Simeon had been the "ringleader" over Levi, his younger brother.

- It is my opinion that Simeon had character issues, which could best be addressed by the Lord under such circumstances as being in a foreign prison.

Character flaws must be dealt with in our lives. The Holy Spirit often chooses to deal with these issues in ways that require that we be boxed in and uncomfortable. When God puts you in a box, the best response is to yield. Don't fight it; hold still and let the Lord operate on you so that you grow with each test.

After removing Simeon from among them, he then instructed them to take the corn which they had bought, and go their way. "Joseph then ordered his servants to fill the men's sacks with grain, but also gave secret instructions to put each brother's payment at the top of his sack! He also gave them provisions for the journey. So they loaded up their donkeys with the grain and started for home. But when they stopped for the night, and one of them opened his sack to get some grain to feed the donkeys, there was his money in the mouth of the sack."[22]

JOSEPH RETURNED THE BROTHER'S PAYMENTS AND ALSO GAVE THEM PROVISIONS FOR THEIR JOURNEY

"'My silver has been returned,' he said to his brothers. 'Here it is in my sack.' Their hearts sank and they turned to each other trembling and said, 'What is this that God has done to us?'"

Upon arriving back in Hebron the sons of Jacob gave a full report to their father. They began to talk over each other trying to make sure that a full accounting was given of all that occurred.

"There is a man who is the governor of all the land of Egypt. This man is the one all foreigners must deal with when purchasing grain. This man "spoke very roughly to us and took us for spies. 'No, no,' we said, 'we are honest men, not spies. We are twelve brothers, sons of one father; one is dead, and the youngest is with our father in the land of Canaan.' Then the man told us, 'This is the way I will find out if you are what you claim to be. Leave one of your brothers here with me and take grain for your families and go on home; but bring your youngest brother back to me. Then I shall know whether you are spies or honest men; if you prove to be what you say, then I will give you back your brother and you can come as often as you like to purchase grain.'"[23]

From their conversation with Jacob they turned toward their sacks of grain to show what they had brought back from

Egypt. "As they were emptying their sacks, there in each man's sack was his pouch of silver! When they and their father saw the money pouches, they were frightened. Their father Jacob said to them, 'You have deprived me of my children. Joseph is no more and Simeon is no more, and now you want to take Benjamin. Everything is against me!'"[24]

All the brothers begged of their father to fear nothing, but to send Benjamin along with them. However, Jacob was not pleased with anything his sons had done.[25]

Reuben took the lead and offered his two sons as collateral for the safe return of Benjamin. He said, "You may put both of my sons to death if I do not bring him back to you. Entrust him to my care, and I will bring him back."[26] But Jacob replied, "My son shall not go down with you, for his brother Joseph is dead and he alone is left of his mother's children. If anything should happen to him, I would die."[27]

They Attempted to do Damage Control

These brothers found themselves in a desperate dilemma. The present conflict and turmoil they were in was because of the wickedness which they were guilty of so long ago. The law of sowing and reaping was bearing down on them and they were losing control.

They tried to do damage control, but they were unable to determine the direction of the wind. They had gotten by without being discovered for these twenty-two years, but payday was quickly approaching and they could not predict anything that was about to happen. Things were about to catch up with them. It was as if they were being torn between five different forces at work in their lives:

* GOD
* The famine
* Zaphnath-paaneah
* Jacob
* Guilt from past sins

They feared that God was making life difficult. This was being driven by the guilt inside their chests. They were pawns of a terrible famine, which was creating the need for them to go to Egypt to find food to survive. The Egyptian ruler, Zaphnath-paaneah, was suspicious of them, and for no legitimate reason. He had become an obstacle which must be responded to if they were to survive the famine. Finally, there was their stubborn father, Jacob, who seemed to love and value only the two sons of Rachel. Even though he had ten other sons and a daughter, he always referred to these two: Joseph and Benjamin.

Nothing would change for this family until old mistakes were corrected and sins were confronted. Each family member must deal with their own indiscretions before peace would return to their lives.

Endnotes

1. Genesis 37:2
2. Genesis 41:46
3. Genesis 45:6
4. Genesis 42:23
5. Josephus, Antiquities, Book 2, 6:2
6. Genesis 42:7 TLB
7. Genesis 42:9 KJV
8. Josephus, Antiquities, Book 2, 6:2
9. Josephus, Antiquities, Book 2,6:2
10. Genesis 42:13 TLB
11. Genesis 42:13 TLB
12. Josephus, Antiquities, Book 2, 6:3
13. Josephus, Antiquities, Book 2, 6:3
14. Josephus, Antiquities, Book 2, 6:3
15. Genesis 49:21-25
16. Genesis 42:14
17. Genesis 42:18-20 TLB
18. Josephus, Antiquities, Book 2, 6:5
19. Luke 12:2-3 AMP
20. Genesis 42:21-24 TLB
21. Genesis 42:19-24
22. Genesis 42:25-27 TLB
23. Genesis 42:30-34 TLB
24. Genesis 42:35-36 NIV
25. Josephus, Antiquities, Book 2, 6:5
26. Genesis 42:37 NIV
27. Genesis 42:38 TLB

Chapter 11

EGYPTIAN HOSPITALITY

The family all hoped for a little reprieve, but there was no relief from the terrible famine throughout the region. When the grain they had brought from Egypt was almost gone, their father said to them, "Go again and buy us a little food."[1]

The first time around, the sons had begged Jacob to send them, but now they could only wait around for him to change his mind. When the grain was almost gone Jacob finally began to hint that they really must do something about their food shortage.

Although there had been no recent discussion about returning to Egypt, Jacob's words demonstrate that he had been thinking about it all during the days and nights. He was stressed. He felt so strongly that he was prepared to react at even the slightest mention of the situation by his sons.

As soon as the subject was brought up, he snapped without hesitation, "Why did you deal so wrongfully with me, as to tell the man whether you had another brother?" It is as if there had been no break in the previous conversation even though weeks and weeks had passed. Clearly, this family had communication issues. They danced around each other, lacking the transparency needed for healthy relationships. As a result of high levels of guilt, there is one common thread running through this family—they remain on slow boil just below the surface, and can easily be set off. It seems that they crossed paths with each other just long enough to deal with necessities, and then retreated to their own respective corners to await the confrontation.

Instantly, the sons of Jacob reacted to their father's accusation by blasting back with these words, "The man asked us pointedly about ourselves and our family saying, 'Is your father still alive? Have you another brother?' And we answered him according to his questions. Could we possibly have known that he would say, 'Bring your brother down'?"

Judah was the one who responded to Jacob's words. He "was of a bold temper on other occasions" and "spoke his mind very freely."[2] Judah said to his father, "The man warned us solemnly, 'You will not see my face again unless your brother is with you.' If you will send our brother along with us, we will go down and buy food for you. But if you will not send him, we will not go down, because the man said to us, 'You will not see my face again unless your brother is with you.'"[3]

> JUDAH SAID, I WILL GUARANTEE BENJAMIN'S SAFETY; IF I DO NOT BRING HIM BACK ... I WILL BEAR THE BLAME BEFORE YOU ALL MY LIFE

Then Judah said to his father, "Send the boy along with me and we will go at once, so that we and you and our children may live and not die. I myself will guarantee his safety; you can hold me personally responsible for him. If I do not bring him back to you and set him here before you, I will bear the blame before you all my life. As it is, if we had not delayed, we could have gone and returned twice."[4]

Finally their father, Jacob, said to them, "If it can't be avoided, then at least do this. Load your donkeys with the best products of the land. Take them to the man as gifts—balm, honey, spices, myrrh, pistachio nuts, and almonds. Take double money so that you can pay back what was in the mouths of your sacks, as it was probably someone's mistake, and take your brother and go. May God Almighty give you mercy before the man, so that he will release Simeon and return Benjamin; and if I must bear the anguish of their deaths, then so be it."[5]

So the men began their long journey with their focus on wasting no time in the way. As soon as they came into Egypt they went directly to the court of Zaphnath-paaneah and presented themselves. They were feeling great fear and were concerned, lest they be accused, in some way, regarding the cost of the corn, as if they had cheated Joseph.[6]

Upon arriving at the court of Zaphnath-paaneah they waited to be received by him. Joseph saw them and Benjamin with them. He did not speak to them, but rather to his steward saying, "Take these men to my house, slaughter an animal and prepare dinner; they are to eat with me at noon."[7]

Immediately upon arriving at the palace they approached the personal steward of Joseph and gave a long apology. They explained that when they had arrived back in Canaan, they had discovered the money in their sacks, and now they were prepared to return it. The steward acted as if he did not know what they meant. Of course they were confused, but at least they were now delivered from that fear.[8] "'We have no idea who put the money in our bag.' The steward said, 'Everything is in order. Don't worry;

your God and the God of your father must have given you a bonus. I was paid in full!' And with that, he presented Simeon to them. He then took them inside Joseph's house and made them comfortable— gave them water to wash their feet and saw to the feeding of their donkeys."[9]

They got their gifts ready to present to Zaphnath-paaneah. When he arrived they bowed low before him and respectfully gave him their gifts.

The Kid Brother is Now Thirty

Benjamin had been about eight years old when Joseph was sold into slavery.[10] At that time, Joseph was seventeen.[11] When Joseph was made governor over Egypt he was thirty years of age.[12] At the time of his reunion with Benjamin, Joseph was thirty-nine. This would have made Benjamin to be a man of about thirty years old.

The eleven brothers exchanged greetings with Joseph. "'And how is your father, the old man you spoke about? Is he still alive?' 'Yes,' they replied, 'He is alive and well!' Then again they bowed before him. Looking at his brother Benjamin, he asked, 'Is this your youngest brother, the one you told me about? How are you, my son? God be gracious to you.' Then Joseph made a hasty exit."[13] Joseph had been "deeply moved at the sight of his brother."[14] As he hurried out Joseph "looked for a place to weep. He went into his private room and wept there. After he had washed his face, he came out and controlling himself, said, 'Serve the food.'"[15]

This great dining room was well equipped for serving many guests. As the brothers looked around the great room, they were amused to see that one table was for Joseph to be seated alone.

They were being directed to a table set only for them; they could see that there were other guests and they sat at a third table.

It became evident to them that, "Egyptians despise Hebrews and never eat with them."[16]

Joseph gave instructions for exactly where each one should sit. This, interestingly enough, was the same order they used for sitting around their father's table.[17]

> JOSEPH GAVE INSTRUCTION FOR EXACTLY WHERE EACH ONE SHOULD SIT ACCORDING TO BIRTH ORDER. HOW DID HE KNOW?

These brothers were amazed because he had made the arrangements almost as if he knew, and had seated them in the order of their ages, from the oldest to the youngest.[18] They looked at one another wide-eyed, wondering what would happen next.[19]

Joseph's table was the master table and all the food was served from it. It was a different custom to these Hebrews as were so many things. When portions were served to them from Joseph's table, Benjamin's portion was five times as much as anyone else's. So they feasted and drank freely with him.[20]

Bounty, Abundance, Too Much! Why? Benjamin was Favored with Five Times as Much

To Benjamin was given such generous servings it was obvious that he was the most honored guest.

Without explanation Benjamin had been singled out to receive five times the volume of food of anyone else at the table. The extravagant hospitality was probably beyond Benjamin's ability to consume; but it did get a point across that Zaphnath-paaneah wished to show special favor to him.

This was a test. Did the brothers harbor jealousy in their hearts for the second born son of Rachel, as they had against the firstborn? If given the opportunity, would they resent him so much they would sell him into slavery, or slay him?

This act of generous hospitality did not go unnoticed by any of these brothers. They saw it; probably stared at it; maybe even laughed out loud, but they did not react. Joseph watched them carefully and felt that they passed the test. He did not detect jealousy, envy, or even resentment. And so the jovial nature of this meal went very well, and the mood was described as merry.[21]

Just One More Test

On the following morning, Joseph gave instructions to his personal steward, "'Fill the men's bags with food—all they can carry—and replace each one's money at the top of the bag. Then put my chalice, my silver chalice, in the top of the bag of the youngest, along with the money for his food.' He did as Joseph ordered."[22]

Joseph conducted this last test of his brothers to see just how loyal they would prove to be if Benjamin were accused of a crime in this land of Egypt; "whether they would stand by Benjamin when he should be accused of having stolen the cup, and should appear to be in danger; or whether they would leave him, and go to their father without him."[23]

HAPPINESS WAS EGYPT IN THEIR REARVIEW MIRROR

Just as the day was about to begin, the brothers of Joseph set off with their donkeys. The journey had only taken them a short distance from the city when Joseph said to his steward, "Go after the Hebrews immediately. When you find them ask, 'Is this how you repay kindness to my Lord, Zaphnath-paaneah? To steal his silver chalice and run away like a common thief? You have done a very wicked thing."[24]

The Hebrew brothers were glad to be back on their way home. They were happily talking and moving as swiftly as they could to get on their way back to Canaan and the Vale of Hebron, where their father would be impatiently waiting for them (and especially for Benjamin and Simeon). They were hoping the famine would end soon, so they would not have to return to Egypt. They felt a double cause of joy, because not only had they been restored to Simeon, but also that they were leaving with their brother Benjamin to take back to their father, without harm.[25] As they moved along, their thoughts were interrupted by a troop of horsemen, who actually encircled them. The only one of these horsemen the brothers recognized was Joseph's personal steward.[26]

THE EGYPTIANS RODE HORSES
THE HEBREWS RODE DONKEYS

Egyptians were renowned in the ancient world as breeders and suppliers of horses. The Egyptian military often rode horses and only horses were used to pull a chariot (never donkeys). To have horses was to substantially increase the mobility of a soldier and therefore to enhance his success in battle.

Israel was warned to put their trust in God and not in horses. Moses had a lot of experience with Egypt and all that it represented. The Lord used Moses to speak a word of wisdom to those Israeli kings who would come in succeeding generations and would be tempted to go to Egypt to enhance their military strength. If they went to Egypt to purchase horses then they would be putting their trust in their own military might. Moses warned future kings:

- **Do not multiply horses**, lest you trust in yourself in battle.

- **Do not multiply wives**, lest your heart be turned away from the Lord.

- **Do not multiply silver and gold,** for it will lead to greed and self-sufficiency.

- **Read the law of God,** and make all laws based on these laws and obey them. [27]

Joseph's brothers had little experience with horses, so when the Egyptian police bore down on them, surrounded them (and that being on horseback) it must have been quite terrifying; hence such significance between Egypt's horses and their donkeys.

The steward began to accuse the Hebrews, just as he had been instructed. He did not miss a word, but raising his voice, fired the accusation with the same intent Joseph had hoped for.

The situation quickly escalated as the brothers, all shocked and taken totally by surprise, reacted.

"'What in the world are you talking about?' they demanded, 'What kind of people do you think we are, that you accuse us of such a terrible thing as that? Didn't we bring back the money we found in the mouth of our sacks? Why would we steal silver or gold from your master's house? If you find his cup with any one of us, let that one die, and all the rest of us will be slaves forever to your master.' 'Fair enough,' the man replied, 'Except that only the one who stole it will be a slave, and the rest of you can go free.'"[28]

It is easy to become cocky, arrogant, or boisterous when you feel you are innocent and in a position of strength.

It is tempting to make big demands when you feel that vindication is inevitable.

These brothers of Joseph were confident that not even one of them would have stolen Joseph's precious silver chalice. Not one of them would have lifted it from the palace of the great Egyptian governor, Zaphnath-paaneah. The gamble would have been too great and the fall-out too much. They were capable of many things, but theft was not in the repertoire of sins they were willing to commit. Besides, yesterday's dinner at the palace had left them feeling grateful that a bad chapter of their lives was about to be over. Why would any of them have even imagined committing such a foolish indiscretion as stealing anything from their host?

> UNRESOLVED SIN WILL LEAVE YOU HANGING AND WITHOUT RECOURSE

Like a runner about to cross the finish line well ahead of his opponents, these brothers were sure they were home free. Unaware of the conspiracy playing out against them, over-confidence was surging through them. But Joseph had a plan. He had to find out just what character traits were lacking in these men. Joseph was out to use the famine, Egypt, and his position as the proving ground to discover just what evil, if any, yet remained in the hearts of these criminals of twenty-two years ago.

Joseph thought to himself, "This desert pit stop is as good a place as any for this final test to begin."

Joseph's steward prepared for the search. "They out did each other in putting their bags on the ground and opening them up for inspection."[29] They lined up from the oldest to the youngest, true to their tradition, as Jacob had trained them well. It must have been interesting for the steward of Joseph to watch, because he had seen their order at the table the day before in Joseph's palace. He began with Reuben's bag. Reuben was careful to observe every move of the steward as he dipped his hands down into the grain to see if the contraband was there. No, it was not in Reuben's bag, but the search did yield something very strange; the pouch of silver, which had been used by Reuben to pay for this grain.[30] Reuben, and all those who saw it must have rolled their eyes to reflect déjà vu. They had been down this same road before. This was so much like what Reuben had been through on his first visit to Egypt; now history was repeating itself.[31]

The Side Effects of Sin

Reuben and each of his brothers had personally struggled with high levels of guilt for twenty-two years. There had probably not been many nights when their guilt did not re-visit them in one way or another.

Here they were, almost out of sight of this very difficult Egyptian ruler's city, and they were having another confrontation. Joseph's personal steward was digging, even at this moment, in Reuben's sack of grain trying to find the silver chalice of his master. The chalice was not found; but the bag of silver, which he had used to pay for this grain, was there. All at once, and for no understandable reason, Reuben felt the pain of guilt. It came as heaviness in his chest. The steward had not found the chalice, and Reuben could not understand how the money was back in his sack. Though Reuben could say whatever he wished, the fact remains that he could not understand why he felt such pangs of guilt, when he had done nothing wrong. What was the reason for this guilt? Sin will defeat you at every turn. Until sin is dealt with in a life, there will never be true peace.

The steward looked up at Reuben; moved on to the sack of Simeon, then the others. Each of them had their own bout with guilt. It just would not go away. Guilt is an inescapable side effect of sin.

Endnotes

1. Genesis 43:1-2 TLB
2. Josephus, Antiquities, Book 2, 6:5
3. Genesis 43:3-5 NIV
4. Genesis 43:8-10 NIV
5. Genesis 43:11-14 TLB
6. Josephus, Antiquities, Book 2, 6:6
7. Genesis 43:16 NIV
8. Josephus, Antiquities, Book 2, 6:6
9. Genesis 43:23-24 MSG
10. Dake's Bible, Page 36, "H"
11. Genesis 37:2
12. Genesis 41:46
13. Genesis 43:27:30 TLB
14. Genesis 43:30 NIV
15. Genesis 43:30 NIV
16. Genesis 43:32 TLB
17. Josephus, Antiquities, Book 2, 6:6
18. Genesis 43:33 TLB
19. Genesis 43:33 MSG
20. Genesis 43:34 NIV
21. Genesis 43:34 NKJV
22. Genesis 44:1-2 MSG
23. Josephus, Antiquities, Book 2, 6:7
24. Paraphrased: Genesis 44:3-5
25. Josephus, Antiquities, Book 2, 6:7
26. Josephus, Antiquities, Book 2, 6:7
27. Paraphrased: Deuteronomy 17:16:20
28. Genesis 44:7-10 TLB
29. Genesis 44:11 MSG
30. Genesis 44:1
31. Genesis 42:25 and 44:2

Chapter 12

THE FINAL TEST

What was the personal steward of Joseph thinking as he watched this continuing drama play out before him?

He must have wondered, "Just what is going on with my master, Zaphnath-paaneah? Why does he harass these Hebrew men?" It must have seemed like Joseph had a vendetta against these ten brothers from Canaan (now eleven since the younger one had come). The steward had worked for Joseph for several years, and had always witnessed his impeccable character. Never in all these years had he seen any inconsistency, until now. The steward must have thought to himself, "Joseph must know something I do not know. He must, being so wise in every area of wisdom, see something I am missing."

In his culture, the steward could never raise a question or query the integrity or judgment of someone as esteemed as Zaphnath-paaneah. This could result in loss of employment on the light end, or even to his being executed; so the drama continued unabated.

The steward had been standing nearby when Joseph first called for an interpreter to assist him in speaking Hebrew to these men; and yet he knew that Joseph could speak several languages—and that Hebrew was his native tongue. This raised several questions in the mind of the steward.

- Why had Joseph chosen not to reveal that he could communicate with them?

- Why had he been so adamant that they were spies? After all, it had now been proven (even to Joseph's satisfaction) that they were, in fact, brothers.

- Why had Joseph ordered him to plant their money back into their respective sacks? Why then had Joseph instructed him to deny any knowledge of this money in their sacks when the brothers made inquiry?

- Why had Joseph felt so sure the brothers would not return to Egypt if he did not imprison one of them (Simeon)?

- Why had Joseph invited the Hebrews to share the noon meal with him in his palace? Why did he feed them so generously, when he did nothing like this for other Canaanites, Moabites, Philistines, or even Arabs?

The generosity of Joseph to these men had been quite amazing. He had insisted that each time their bags were filled with grain they must be filled so full they could hardly be carried.

As a matter of fact, from where the steward sat, it seemed that neither their first visit or second visit to purchase grain had cost them even one piece of silver—they had actually come to Egypt for free food when everyone else had to pay a premium.

Maybe one reason Joseph had kept Simeon in prison was to create opportunity to continue to bless them.

It was confusing to the steward. Now the latest instruction from Joseph was to plant the silver cup in the sack of the youngest one. How would this work out? What did Joseph have in mind? What was he so suspicious of concerning them?

> IT SEEMED TO THE STEWARD THAT THESE TRIPS TO EGYPT HAD COST THEM NOTHING AT ALL

The steward was intrigued. He felt it best to keep his mouth shut and his eyes and ears open. He was about to learn a great lesson from Zaphnath-paaneah, and he did not want to miss the moment when the truth was revealed.

The steward knew something was going on in the mind of Zaphnath-paaneah, but he was not yet sure where it was going to lead. Fully aware of where the cup was, he continued his methodical search in order, finishing with Reuben and proceeding with Simeon. He may have even felt amusement at the responses of these men, and must certainly have wondered what the real story was behind it all.

The search of Simeon's sack yielded no silver chalice, but the pouch of silver alone. Of course the steward knew just where he would find the cup because he had put it there himself. It would be in Benjamin's sack. As he exposed the money in Simeon's sack he looked up and into his eyes, then moved on to the next brother.[1] He almost imagined that he could see it for a moment—there it was—guilt, in the eyes of Simeon. Although the steward knew this man had not stolen the money, his eyes seemed to reveal an inner pain of some kind.

He finished searching the sacks belonging to Levi, then Judah, then Dan, Naphtali, Gad, Asher, Issachar, and then Zebulun. The steward stopped for a moment to brace for the inevitable, savoring the drama. He knew the next bag he searched would be that of the youngest brother, Benjamin.

EACH BROTHER REACHED HIS HAND TO HIS COLLAR AND TORE HIS CLOTHES IN DEEP DESPAIR AND GRIEF

And so, he stepped in front of Benjamin. Lying there just under a few inches of grain was the corner of the cup. He drew it out, lifting it for all to see.[2]

To the amazement of the steward, in one movement, these brothers each reached their hands to the collar of his garment; tearing, in shreds the very clothes he was wearing. He had seen this before, but only when someone had died. This family was experiencing trauma, sadness and deep despair like he had never seen before.[3]

The horsemen quickly stepped forward taking custody of Benjamin. They assumed the authority over the situation, in effect pushing the steward aside. Binding the hands of Benjamin they placed him on his donkey to be forcibly removed from this place and delivered back to the governor of Egypt.

These men took charge so quickly that Benjamin's brothers had to rush to pull themselves together so that they did not get separated from the steward and the guards.[4]

The horsemen wasted no time making their delivery to the governor. Nothing was said to the Hebrews as they moved en masse to the palace of Joseph, for he was yet there: They threw themselves down on the ground in front of him[5]

"Joseph said to them, 'What is this you have done? Don't you know that a man like me can find things out by divination?'"[6] "Didn't you know such a man as I would know who stole it?"[7]

The Silver Divining Cup

Joseph's use of the word divination impressed upon the brothers that he was genuinely an Egyptian. Divining cups were used among the Egyptians as well as other nations. They bore certain magical inscriptions.[8]

It is unlikely that Joseph actually used it for divination because of his personal commitment to God; but it certainly was an effective tool to portray himself as Egyptian, in contrast to Hebrew custom.

It was Judah who began to speak. "What can we say, master? What is there to say? How can we prove our innocence? God is behind this, exposing how bad we are. We stand guilty before you and ready to be your slaves—we're all in this together, the rest of us as guilty as the one with the chalice." Joseph responded, "I'd never do that to you. Only the one involved with the chalice will be my slave. The rest of you are free to go back to your father."[9]

Joseph made it clear that he was dismissing the ten brothers for they were guilty of no offense; and that he must now be content with seeing to the lad's punishment; for it was not right to release a guilty man as it would send the wrong message when considering justice. He also could not consider punishing all of them, as they were suggesting. They must now take their grain, with their donkeys and return to Canaan and their father.[10]

However, Judah, in sincere humility, persisted further, by coming near to Joseph. He said, "Please, master; may I say just one thing to you? Don't get angry. Don't think I'm presumptuous—

JUDAH SPOKE TO THE EGYPTIAN RULER IN SINCERE HUMILITY

you're the same as Pharaoh as far as I'm concerned. You, master, asked us, 'Do you have a father and a brother?' And we answered honestly, 'We have a father who is old and a younger brother who was born to him in his old age. His brother is dead and he is the only son left from that mother. And his father loves him more than anything.'"

"Then you told us, 'Bring him down here so I can see him.' We told you, 'Master, that is not possible: The boy can't leave his father; if he leaves, his father will die.' And then you said, 'If your youngest brother doesn't come with you, you won't be allowed to see me.'"

"When we returned to our father, we told him everything you said to us. So when our father said, 'Go back and buy some more food,' we told him flatly, 'We can't. 'The only way we can go back is if our youngest brother is with us. We aren't allowed to even see the man if our youngest brother doesn't come with us.'"[11]

It was Judah's Time to Repent

This was the hour for Judah to make things right. It had been Judah who had said to the others, "Here come some Ishmaelites. Let's sell Joseph to them! Why kill him and have a guilty conscience? Let's not be responsible for his death, for, after all, he is our brother!"[12]

Even though Judah's words had saved Joseph from death, in one way, it had released him into the unknown world of human trafficking.[13] As it happened, during these last twenty-two years they had to think of Joseph as now being dead. What Judah had done on that day had complicated an already bad situation. The fear of the unknown had created a sense of being cursed and haunted with guilt in their subconscious souls.

This was the time for Judah to purge his heart, confess his sins, and do the right thing—for once.

In all this time, nothing good had ever come out of what these brothers had done to Joseph. How they longed to reclaim the past and erase their guilt, but it would never be possible.

Judah recognized that the next best thing was to save Benjamin. He must not let evil come to his younger brother. He saw the path before him and made his decision. He would plead guilty and cast himself before Zaphnath-paaneah, trusting in whatever goodness this Egyptian ruler might possess. Judah saw himself as being guilty of more than he could ever say and felt he must become Benjamin's substitute for Jacob's sake, if not also for Joseph's sake. Justice had been a long time coming, but Judah was prepared. He could live no longer without redemption.

JUDAH OFFERED HIMSELF AS BENJAMIN'S SUBSTITUTE

Redemption Brings a Great Cleansing

The need for redemption is a powerful force. It invades the thought life of anyone guilty of secret sins. There came a point in the life of Judah where he felt his entire family must be redeemed if they were ever again to come to any good. The present circumstances left them with no recourse, so he must step forward and take the place of his innocent brother, Benjamin.

Judah continued saying to Joseph, "Please realize that our father then drew us close and reminded us that Rachel, the boy's mother, had given him two sons. One just disappeared and was

113

probably ripped to pieces by a wild animal. He is still grieving that
he has never seen him since that time."[14] Judah quoted his father
by saying, "If you take this one from me too and harm comes to
him, you will bring my grey head down to the grave in misery."[15]

"So now, can't you see that if I show up before your servant,
my father, without the boy, this son with whom his life is so
bound up; the moment he realizes the boy is gone, he'll die
on the spot? He'll die of grief and we, your servants who are
standing here before you, will have killed him. And that's not
all. I got my father to release the boy to show him to you by
promising, 'If I don't bring him back, I'll stand condemned
before you, Father, all my life.'"

"So, let me stay here as your slave, not the boy. Let the boy
go back with his brothers. How can I go back to my father if
the boy is not with me?[16] I cannot bear to see what this would
do to him."[17]

Joseph's Dreams Come to Pass

Joseph was now satisfied that he was witnessing ten changed
brothers. They were no longer envious or jealous. They had
experienced so much guilt that they were repentant for all
they had done. Joseph recognized their true remorse for the
wickedness of their youth, and how different they were in their
love and respect for Benjamin.

In the heart and soul of Joseph, he felt that he had been
separated from his family too long. He had longed for fellowship
with them for years and now felt he could surely trust them at
last. Because of the envy, jealousy, hatred, and treachery of his
brothers, Joseph had never really benefited from family fun and

normal conversation. For the first time he felt that he could open up his heart and become vulnerable to them.

Joseph braced himself and said the words which he'd rehearsed over and over in the dark of the night. How he had longed to see this moment and had believed that it surely would come to pass!

> JOSEPH HAD ALWAYS BELIEVED THAT GOD WOULD BRING HIS DREAMS TO PASS

The Lord had given him two dreams long ago. Now, as Joseph observed these eleven men before him, he realized that his dreams had been totally accurate. They were being fulfilled right before his eyes. He had been elevated to be ruler over the land and they bowed low before him. He did not evaluate these dreams to enhance his greatness or their lowliness, but rather as an acknowledgement of the plan and purpose of God.

Throughout the years, Joseph's faith had remained buoyant only because he trusted in four things:

* "Joseph knew that his dreams were RIGHT.
* He knew that his dreams were REAL.
* He knew that God was still on the throne,
* and that God would bring his dreams to pass."[18]

This confidence had sustained him through difficult times. Now, in the ninth year of his governorship over Egypt, God's purpose had been fulfilled. Panic, horror, and fear came to a crescendo in the emotion of these Hebrews as Joseph revealed himself to them.

Endnotes ⸻

1. Paraphrased: Josephus, Antiquities, Book 2, 6; 7
2. Paraphrased: Josephus, Antiquities, Book 2, 6:7
3. Genesis 44:13
4. Josephus, Antiquities, Book 2, 6:7
5. Genesis 44:14 MSG
6. Genesis 44:15 NIV
7. Genesis 44:15 TLB
8. Dake's Bible, Page 44, "K"
9. Genesis 44:16-17 MSG
10. Paraphrased: Josephus, Antiquities, Book 2, 6:8
11. Genesis 44:18-26 MSG
12. Genesis 37:27 TLB
13. Google "Human Trafficking" for your own research in the 21st century.
14. Paraphrased: Genesis 44:27-28
15. Genesis 44:29 NIV
16. Genesis 44:30-34 MSG
17. Genesis 44:34 TLB
18. I heard Zig Ziglar say this in a speech in a live talk. Zig Ziglar Corporate Headquarters, 5055 West Park Boulevard, Suite 700, Plano, TX 75093

PANIC ATTACK

Joseph could stand it no longer.[1] He was no longer able to act like he was an angry man.[2] He had to clear the hall of anyone but his family.

Joseph cried out, as if he were in pain and deep anguish, ordering, "Out, all of you... and he was left alone with his brothers. Then he wept aloud. His sobs could be heard throughout the great hall, and the news was quickly carried to Pharaoh's palace."

Joseph was preparing to make himself known to his brothers and he felt that this sacred moment must be done with them alone.[3]

"Joseph spoke to his brothers: 'I am Joseph. Is my father really still alive?' But they could not say a word. They were speechless— they couldn't believe what they were hearing and seeing.'"[4]

On every occasion when Joseph had dealt with these brothers; whether it was in his court, in his home at the noon meal, or now at his palace, Joseph had used his interpreter to communicate.

His words had always been quiet, with the interpreter making the loud boisterous demands. Now for the first time, Joseph emerged from his quiet posture to speak directly to them. The last thing he said in the Egyptian tongue was to order everyone but the eleven brothers from the room. He had said, "Leave. Everyone go from here immediately. Cause every man to go out from me."[5]

When Joseph had abruptly cleared the room he had spoken in the Egyptian language. These Hebrews would not have understood what was going on. Perhaps they had even wondered if he was angry with them and if things were going to go from bad to worse.

> WHEN JOSEPH SPOKE, THEIR HEARTS WERE FILLED WITH ABSOLUTE TERROR FOR A FEW MOMENTS

Joseph stopped. He looked directly into the eyes of these men (who were most likely still bowing before him). He composed himself, cleared his throat, and proceeded. By this time the brother's sad demeanor had moved from quizzical, to concern, then to absolute terror.

"I am Joseph. Is my father really still alive?"[6]

"Come closer to me."[7] Joseph said to his brothers. They numbly jostled closer. "I am Joseph your brother, whom you sold into Egypt! But don't be angry at yourselves that you did this to me, for God did it! He sent me here ahead of you to preserve your lives. These two years of famine will grow to seven, during which there will be neither plowing nor harvest. God has sent me here to keep you and your families alive, so that you will become a great nation. Yes, it was God who sent me here, not you! And he has made me a counselor to Pharaoh, and manager of this entire nation, ruler of all the land of Egypt."[8]

It is hard to imagine the human emotion experienced at that very moment there in the court of the great Egyptian governor. These ten brothers were in the battle of their lives to free Benjamin from slavery. Judah was standing before the judicial authority of the governor pleading for him to allow Benjamin to return to Canaan to be with his aging father, Jacob. At the same time he was begging for permission to stand in for Benjamin, as his substitute. Judah was desperate to redeem his younger brother from slavery. He had just said, in his closing plea: "Please sir, let me stay here as a slave instead of the lad, and let the lad return with his brothers."[9]

Joseph's revelation had hit these eleven men in about the same way as if a pyramid had fallen out of the sky. They blinked their eyes. They examined every facial characteristic. They listened to his excellent grasp of Hebrew ... and then the fearsome reality hit them. Could it possibly be? Yes—this man is Joseph. It took some moments to really sink in.

THESE BROTHERS WERE ABSOLUTELY SPEECHLESS AS JOSEPH SPOKE

Could it be that through all the occasions when they'd had interaction with Zaphnath-paaneah—Joseph—they had not detected any resemblance? None of these Hebrew brothers had even had a clue of his identity? Of course, he had been rather quiet and they had only heard the voice of the steward and the interpreter, but still ... what a surprise, what a shock!

In that moment, their long struggle with guilt turned into fear—fear of reprisal, fear of Joseph's revenge, and finally, fear of Jacob's response when he found out the truth. Once before they had wondered, now they wondered again. "They looked at one another wide eyed, wondering what would happen next."[10]

If any of these older brothers had ulcers, now was surely the time for them to act up. They felt anxiety—the fear of being on the hot seat and unable to predict what would come next. What level of retribution would be their fate?

Joseph said, "So now it was not you who sent me here, but God and He has made me a father to Pharaoh, and Lord of all his house, and a ruler throughout all the land of Egypt."[11]

Joseph, a Father to Pharaoh

"God… has made me a father to Pharaoh."[12] Throughout Egypt there are many monuments of its ancient rulers. Some historians suggest that this Pharaoh was the one named Apepi, and that he was actually somewhat younger than Joseph. If this is true he had only been Pharaoh for a short time, having succeeded his father. He was the third generation of Pharaohs from his dynasty.

This would certainly explain why Joseph, at age thirty-nine, was a father figure to Pharaoh.[13] Perhaps Pharaoh's youth caused him to be even more willing and glad to have a man of such wisdom as Joseph to assume oversight of his household and the nation.

It seems quite clear that Joseph had become even more than an adviser, but also a mentor and a father to this young king.

Joseph, a Brother among Brothers

Joseph enjoyed the fellowship he had with his brothers. It was precious to savor this time of just being in close proximity with his family, from whom he had been so long estranged.

He spoke seriously now to his brothers. They were just now being reacquainted after twenty-two years, and in some respects acquainted for the first time. Joseph urged his brothers to quickly leave Egypt to fetch their father for a speedy return to the bounty, which Egypt offered them.

"Go quickly to my father. Tell him, his son, Joseph is alive, well, and blessed here in this land of Egypt. Tell him that the Lord has preserved me here and I am waiting for him to speedily come to be with me."[14]

Tell him, "Your son Joseph says: 'I'm master of all of Egypt. Come as fast as you can and join me here. I'll give you a place to live in Goshen where you'll be close to me; you, your children, your grandchildren, your flocks, your herds, and anything else you can think of. I'll take care of you there completely. There are still five more years of famine ahead. I'll make sure your needs are taken care of, you and everyone connected with you; you won't want for a thing.'"[15]

WHAT WOULD JACOB SAY TO HIS SONS WHEN HE HEARD THE NEWS OF JOSEPH?

"Otherwise, you will come to utter poverty along with all your household."[16] "Tell my father all about the high position I hold in Egypt, tell him everything you've seen here, but don't take all day. Hurry up and get my father down here."[17]

Then, weeping with joy, he embraced Benjamin who began weeping as well. Joseph did the same with each of his brothers, renewing his relationship with each one of them. Finally everything loosened up and all of them talked freely with Joseph, as they could see clearly the sincerity of his heart.[18]

When the news reached Pharaoh's palace that Joseph's brothers had come, Pharaoh and all his officials were pleased. Pharaoh said to Joseph, "Do this: load your animals and return to the land of Canaan, and bring your father and your families back to me. I will give you the best of the land of Egypt and you can enjoy the fat of the land."[19] Pharaoh was especially glad to respond to Joseph's family, feeling almost, "… as if it had been a part of his own good fortune; and gave them wagons full of corn, and gold and silver, to be conveyed to his father."[20]

"So Joseph followed through and gave them wagons, as Pharaoh had commanded, and provisions for the journey."[21] Generosity flowed from the house of Pharaoh, even to the very clothes they were wearing. Each of Joseph's brothers was given new clothes, which were to be admired.

Extravagant Blessing

This was generosity like they had never seen.[22] More gifts were given to Benjamin than to the others, so great was the favor shown to him.[23]

The principle of generosity had been firmly established in the life of Joseph and now in the life of Benjamin. The favor of God was evident in how Benjamin was treated. Joseph had activated this principle by serving Benjamin five times as much food as the brothers.[24] Now, to each of the brothers he gave several complete changes of garments, but he took it a step further by giving added blessing to Benjamin. He gave to Benjamin extravagant blessing by giving to him three hundred pieces of silver and five changes of raiment.[25]

Jealousy had been a problem when Joseph was young, but it seems that these brothers had been through so much that they no longer allowed themselves to be bitten by this serpent. They had seen what heartache comes with being jealous. They seem quite glad to accommodate the favor and blessing which was coming to Benjamin.

Pharaoh also insisted that Joseph show his generosity by saying to them, "Take wagons from Egypt to carry your little ones and your wives and load up your father and come back. Don't worry about having to leave things behind; the best in all of Egypt will be yours."[26]

Heaven's Passport is Greater than Earth's

It is a beautiful thing to receive such a promise as Jacob received from Pharaoh, "Don't worry about having to leave things behind; the best in all of Egypt will be yours."[27]

When you give your heart to the Lord, then you add strength to your claim to being a member of the human race. The new claim is that you are a part of the Family of God. When you're a member of the Family of God then you are blessed with the rights and privileges, as well as the heavenly citizenship of the Kingdom of heaven. Your best passport is not with one of the earthly governments of this world, but you become, in advance, a citizen of heaven.

The Lord will bless those who are His own. This world does not understand this kind of talk. Actually they resent it, because they have not received a revelation of who the Lord Jesus Christ really is. They'd rather take Him down from the throne and take His name in vain than to give Him the glory He deserves. There is an afterlife. Certain decisions must be made now, while living in this life, so that we are fully prepared for our eternity with the Lord.

Pharaoh opened his heart to be generous to Jacob and his family. He accepted the Hebrews as favored citizens and guests of his government. This kind of favor only comes to those whom the Lord has chosen to bless.

God Will Settle What He Owes You

When you are called to serve the Lord, you must open up your heart to a higher level of personal commitment than you would if you just join a club and are given a membership card.

When you are called into Christian service (to commit yourself and even your family to serve the Lord in a leadership capacity) then it may be that you will be called on to make sacrifices. Often, especially when that calling involves ministry or mission work in another part of the country or the world, you will find yourself making personal sacrifices from family and friends and assets.

Occasionally, the sacrifice will involve leaving your parents, children, and grandchildren for several years at a time to serve the Lord on a mission field in some other nation. These levels of sacrifice can come at a great personal cost. When Jesus was dealing with the rich young ruler,[28] the subject moved from, "What shall I do to inherit eternal life;"[29] to Jesus' challenge to him, since he had obeyed the commandments, to take the next step. Jesus said to this young man, "You still lack one thing. Sell everything you have and give to the poor, and you will have treasure in heaven. Then come, follow me."[30]

The rich young ruler left in disappointment, because he was a man of great wealth.[31] As the conversation continued between Jesus and his disciples, Peter brought the subject around to the level of Christian service by saying, "We have left all we had to follow you!"[32]

Jesus responded to Peter by saying to all the disciples, "I tell you the truth, no one who has left home or wife or brothers or parents or children for the sake of the kingdom of God will fail to receive many times as much in this age and, in the age to come, eternal life."[33]

It was significant that Pharaoh said to these sons of Jacob, "Don't worry about having to leave things behind; the best in all of Egypt will be yours."[34]

It must be realized that God will always repay his debts. If you give to God, you can be assured that He will make it up to you. Your repayment may be in kind (meaning money for money, houses for houses) or in principle (meaning divine protection, good health, long life, or divine favor over your household). You will only know the full divine response as you enter eternal life. Know also that after a life of service, you can look back over the landscape of your life and discover countless blessings, benefits, advantages, perks, and serendipities which were only made possible because of God's divine and extravagant favor.

Joseph Was a Giver ... This Made the Difference

These brothers were shocked when Joseph broke into Hebrew the first time, revealing his true identity. They watched closely to judge his sincerity. Each man had to decide for himself whether Joseph really was sincere; otherwise they could not progress to a level of actually trusting him. Joseph not only revealed his true identity but he carefully explained why he was not bitter, why he was not angry, why he had forgiven them, and how he felt that God had been behind his real purpose for coming to Egypt.

Joseph explained all about why God caused him to be in Egypt—to become a counselor and even like a father to

Pharaoh.[35] He went into details about how long the famine would last.[36]

Still the brothers were suspicious of Joseph and could not calm their personal fears. "His brothers were not able to answer him, because they were terrified at his presence,"[37] and greatly troubled.[38]

However, as Joseph's body language showed tears, and weeping, and forgiveness they began to slowly respond to him. He reached out to them to embrace them.[39]

Then he began to give to them. His gifts were everything from hugs and words of kindness to a show of forgiveness. He kissed them. He touched them. He gave them gold, silver, a new wardrobe, and lavish gifts for them to give to his father, Jacob.

They saw his words as comforting and his manner as confirming his sincerity, but it was at the point when he validated it all with his absolute generosity that the rock began to break. Their hearts began to tenderize and the barriers fell down when Joseph began to give.

IT WAS JOSEPH'S GIVING THAT MADE THE REAL DIFFERENCE

Josephus said it this way: "… the generous kindness of their brother seemed to leave among them no room for fear."[40]

Joseph was in a position of strength and wanted to bless his father with a picture of Egypt's prosperity. He gathered as many things together as he could; treasures he carefully selected and flavors, which would cause Jacob's taste buds to dance. He then loaded these precious gifts on ten donkeys; then on ten female donkeys, he loaded, grain, bread, and food for his father for the journey.[41]

Then Joseph sent his brothers on their way and gave them one last encouragement as they departed, "Take it easy on the journey, try to get along with each other."[42] Given their history, this was appropriate advice.

They left Egypt and went back to their father Jacob in Canaan. When they told him, "Joseph is still alive—and he's the ruler over the whole land of Egypt..." he went numb. He couldn't believe his ears! But the more they talked, telling him everything that Joseph had told them, and when he saw the wagons that Joseph had sent to carry him back, the blood started to flow again—and Jacob's spirit revived. Jacob said, "I've heard enough—my son Joseph is still alive. I've got to go and see him before I die."[43]

Endnotes

1. Genesis 45:1 TLB
2. Paraphrase: Josephus, Antiquities, Book 2, 6:9
3. Genesis 45:1
4. Genesis 45:3 TLB
5. Paraphrased: Genesis 45:1
6. Genesis 45:3 TLB
7. Genesis 45:4 NIV
8. Genesis 45:4-8 TLB
9. Genesis 44:33 TLB
10. Genesis 43:33 MSG
11. Genesis 45:8 NKJV
12. Genesis 45:8 NKJV
13. Genesis 45:8
14. Paraphrased: Genesis 45:9-12
15. Genesis 45:9-12 MSG
16. Genesis 45:12 TLB
17. Genesis 45:13 MSG
18. Paraphrased: Genesis 45:15
19. Genesis 45:16-18 NIV
20. Paraphrased: Josephus, Antiquities, Book 2, 6:9
21. Genesis 45:21 TLB
22. Paraphrased: Genesis 45:22
23. Paraphrased: Josephus, Antiquities, Book 2, 6:9
24. Genesis 43:34
25. Genesis 45:22 KJV
26. Genesis 45:19-20 MSG
27. Genesis 45:20 MSG
28. Luke 18:18-23
29. Luke 18:18 KJV
30. Luke 18:22 NIV
31. Luke 18:23 NIV
32. Luke 18:28 NIV
33. Luke 18:29-30 NIV
34. Genesis 45:20 MSG
35. Genesis 45
36. Genesis 45:6
37. Genesis 45:3 NIV
38. Genesis 45:3 KJV
39. Genesis 45:14-15
40. Josephus, Antiquities, Book 2, 6:9
41. Genesis 45:23 NKJV
42. Genesis 45:24 MSG
43. Genesis 45:25-28 MSG

Chapter 14

EGYPT
OR
BUST

Jacob set out with his family and all his descendants and came to the Well of the Oath, which is in Beersheba. There he offered sacrifices to God. These days had been good and certainly the news of Joseph being alive and so prosperous was especially welcomed. However, there were deep concerns in Jacob's heart.

- He was afraid that his children, his grandchildren, and all those who should descend from him and grow up in Egypt, might be tempted by its prosperity and fall in love with it and settle in it. They might not think of returning to the land of Canaan; after all, their heritage was to be found in Canaan, as God had promised them.[1]

- Although it may well have been the will of God for Joseph to relocate to Egypt (because of the noble call in his life), was it the will of God for him to come based only on Joseph's invitation? If he were to make this move to live in Egypt (however right it may seem in view of the circumstances) "... without the will of God, his family might be destroyed there."² With all this on his mind Jacob fell asleep.

During the night, God spoke to him in a vision:

"Jacob, Jacob!" He called.

"Yes?" Jacob answered.

"I am God, the God of your father. Don't be afraid to go down to Egypt; for I will go down with you into Egypt and I will bring your descendants back again; but you shall die in Egypt with Joseph at your side."

Jacob's Dream

Josephus, in his writings, gave insight into the night vision which Jacob experienced while at Beersheba. The Lord addressed the fears of Jacob by making references to events which had taken place throughout his life, using them to confirm what he was presently doing as he led Jacob to relocate from Canaan to Egypt.

"I have been a protector and helper to your forefathers and now for you. Even when your father, Isaac would have deprived you of the dominion, I gave it to you; and it was by My kindness that you were sent into Mesopotamia all alone and that you obtained good wives and returned with much wealth. Your whole family has been preserved by my providence; and it was I who conducted Joseph, your son, to the joy of great prosperity, even though you gave him up for lost. I also made him lord of Egypt, so that he differs but little from a king. Accordingly, I come now to you to guide you in this journey; and foretell that you will die in the arms of Joseph; and I inform you that your posterity shall be many ages

GOD WAS FAITHFUL IN THE PAST AND WOULD BE FAITHFUL FOR THE FUTURE

in authority and glory, and that I will settle them in Canaan, the land which I have promised them."[3]

Jacob awakened encouraged by his dream. As a result, his journey was a happier one, as he was better equipped to face the future and all that this transition would bring.[4]

GOD SPOKE TO JACOB IN THE NIGHT

"So Jacob left Beersheba, and his sons brought him to Egypt, along with their little ones and their wives, in the wagons Pharaoh had provided for them. They brought their livestock too, and all their belongings accumulated in the land of Canaan, and came to Egypt—Jacob and all his children, sons and daughters, grandsons and granddaughters—all his loved ones."[5]

"The total number of those going to Egypt, of his own descendants, not counting the wives of Jacob's sons, was sixty-six. With Joseph and his two sons included, this total of Jacob's household there in Egypt totaled seventy."[6]

Jacob sent Judah on ahead of the family to get directions on how to find Goshen. When all of this company finally arrived Joseph had met them along the way, in his chariot. Upon meeting, Joseph threw his arms around his father and wept for a long time.[7] "Jacob said to Joseph, 'Now let me die, since I have seen your face, because you are still alive.'"[8]

Jacob was exhausted from the long journey and grew faint at the point when he came face to face with Joseph. Joseph impressed upon Jacob the need to get in no hurry, but to travel on slowly.[9]

Joseph was so pleased to meet those who were of Jacob's household. He then gathered the family leaders together and said, "I'll go and tell Pharaoh that my brothers and my father's family, all of whom lived in Canaan, have come to me." He then continued saying, "I would like to take five of my brothers with me as I go to visit Pharaoh."

As Joseph spoke with his brothers he coached them saying, "When Pharaoh calls you in and asks what kind of work you do, tell him, 'Your servants have always kept livestock for as long as we can remember—we and our parents also!' That way he'll let you stay apart in the land of Goshen—for Egyptians look down on anyone who is a shepherd."[10]

Egyptians were Strongly Prejudiced Against Shepherds

Egyptians looked down on anyone who was a shepherd.[11] They felt that all shepherds were detestable[12] and were an abomination unto the Egyptians,[13] even to the point of refusing to eat bread with them.[14]

Joseph knew how the general populous felt about shepherds, so he recognized that it would be a wise thing to avoid conflict by keeping them separate from the Egyptians. "It was a race prejudice not a class prejudice. On the Egyptian monuments shepherds are always depicted as dirty, unshaven or deformed, and as an inferior people. Egypt was an agricultural and commercial country and highly civilized, while shepherds were nomads and rough-like peoples held in contempt."[15]

Joseph and five of his brothers left from Goshen, near the city of Heliopolis,[16] and traveled to the palace of Pharaoh. He always had free access to come before Pharaoh, so he came immediately in to the court of Pharaoh to speak with him about the arrival of his father and his family.

Joseph brought in his five brothers whom he had brought to meet Pharaoh. Joseph said, "My father and my brothers are here from Canaan, with all their flocks and herds and possessions. They wish to settle in the land of Goshen."

Pharaoh spoke with them asking, "What is your occupation?" Their reply was, "We are shepherds like our ancestors. We have come to live here in Egypt, for there is no pasture for our flocks in Canaan—the famine is very bitter there. We request permission to live in the land of Goshen."

Pharaoh said to Joseph, "Choose anywhere you like for them to live.[17] Egypt welcomes them. Settle your father and brothers on the choicest land—yes, give them Goshen. And if you know any among them that are especially good at their work, put them in charge of my own livestock."[18]

Jacob Blessed Pharaoh
Protocol was Left at the Door

Soon Joseph made arrangements and brought his father to meet Pharaoh at the palace. Jacob, upon meeting Pharaoh, immediately extended his hand and prayed a prayer of blessing upon Pharaoh, saluted him, and wished all prosperity to his government.

Jacob's manner and complete social style were against the accepted protocol of Egypt and royalty. Then again, not every guest was as old as this man, Jacob. Pharaoh, being younger, was especially intrigued with Jacob's 130 years.

It is amazing what age does to an individual. The one who is aged is aware of a mature perspective, and has some great insight, wisdom, and experience. The young, who are so much less experienced, are often amused at one who has lived so long.

JACOB WAS FROM THE HILL COUNTRY

HIS AGE TRUMPED THEIR PROTOCOL

Protocol is a rigid set of rules made up by those who serve royalty, high-ranking officials, and VIP's. These rules are, by design, inflexible and unwavering. However, on this occasion, protocol is set aside in favor of genuine communication between Pharoah and Jacob. In deference to his many years and relationship to Joseph, Pharoah was willing to bend and adjust these rules, extending grace and dismissing any repercussions usually caused by a break in protocol. Society in general, and government leaders in particular, can be guilty of taking the rules of protocol so seriously, they forget who they really are and from where they came. In this case, Pharaoh was so amused and impressed with Jacob's years that no concern was given to doing things according to protocol.

After this blessing, Pharaoh just stared at Jacob and asked, "Please tell me, how old are you?"[19]

Jacob, never the one to be shy, leaned back and said, "The years of my pilgrimage are a hundred and thirty. My years have been few and difficult, and they do not equal the years of the pilgrimage of my fathers."[20]

Jacob, once again, blessed Pharaoh.

Jacob Knew the Value of Blessing

Pharaoh was fascinated with the way this ancient man was free with his pronouncements. Being so much younger, Pharaoh found Jacob to be *extremely* old, but beyond his age there was something else about him that amazed Pharaoh.

Jacob was a man of blessing. He had actually walked into the court of Pharaoh much differently than any guest before him. Jacob walked in and blessed Pharaoh, asking nothing in return.

In a world where those who curse are all around us, it is refreshing to encounter someone who blesses. Jacob was a man who, with the spirit of a Patriarch, spoke positive, "destiny things" over those he met. He was a man who revoked the evil forces that were at work in a life, then activated the good things, the wholesome ways, the Godly forces and the positive destiny. Jacob was a man who was not beaten down, despondent, hateful or full of venom; he was a man who took charge and walked in the power and might of the spirit of God. He was an enforcer, an encourager; a man of God who was prophetic and anointed with love; had the nature of redemption in his own nature,

> JACOB GAVE PHARAOH THE FEELING OF FORGIVENESS JUST BY WALKING INTO THE ROOM

and gave Pharaoh the feeling of forgiveness just by walking into the room. The twenty first century needs people like this walking around, touching our lives.

Jacob was not normal, he was better than normal. To a man such as Pharaoh, Jacob must have seemed rather otherworldly. It was a good day for Pharaoh when Joseph's family came to Egypt. He must have thought, "We need more people in Egypt who are just like Jacob."

Then Pharaoh gave Jacob leave to rejoin his family in the area of Ramses and Goshen. They would live in the beautiful and fertile area of Goshen away from the city. For them it should be a good life and a peaceful life.

Joseph made his family his own responsibility throughout the famine, providing for them according to the number of children.[21]

The first journey to Egypt by Joseph's ten brothers cost them nothing, because the steward had returned all their money in their sacks of grain.[22]

It cost nothing for Simeon to live in Egypt, because the government of Pharaoh had paid for his food while he was their guest in the prison.[23]

The second journey by the brothers, plus Benjamin, cost them nothing. Again the steward, acting upon Joseph's instruction, gave back all their money in their sacks of grain.[24]

When they went back to Canaan, they were actually loaded down with priceless gifts to take back to their father. As a result they turned a profit and made money.[25]

JOSEPH WAS RESPONSIBLE FOR ALL THE COST

GOD PAID ALL THE BILLS

Now, when they finally arrived in Egypt to take residency, Joseph assumed personal responsibility of the entire clan to care for their nourishment for the remaining five years of the famine.[26]

This family remained in Egypt for 430 years[27] before Moses repatriated them back to Canaan. Although their exodus was not without a lot of drama, just notice that the Egyptians, once again, opened up their hearts and their treasury to bless these Hebrews financially and in nearly every possible way.[28]

It is a beautiful picture of how God was determined to bless these Hebrews (who came to be known as Israelites, or Israelis).

- The famine cost them nothing.

- They were given priceless gifts as they made a move to Egypt and took up residency.

- They were paid out, as they went through the Exodus, by the generosity of the Egyptians.

- All during the 40 years of the wilderness wanderings God cared for their food by giving them manna, and at times even quail.[29]

Moses spoke wisdom, saying, "If you fully obey all of these commandments of the Lord your God, the laws I am declaring to you today, God will transform you into the greatest nation in the world. These are the blessings that will come upon you:

- Blessings in the city,

- Blessings in the field;

- Many children,

- Ample crops,

- Large flocks and herds;

- Blessings of fruit and bread;

- Blessings when you come in,

- Blessings when you go out.[30]

The Lord will defeat your enemies before you; they will march out together against you, but scatter before you in seven directions! The Lord will bless you with good crops and healthy cattle, and will prosper everything you do when you arrive in the land the Lord your God is giving you. He will change you into a holy people dedicated to God; this He has promised to do if you will only obey Him and walk in His ways. All the nations in the world shall see that you belong to the Lord, and they will stand in awe.

The Lord will give you an abundance of good things in the land, just as He promised: many children, many cattle, and

THE LORD WILL MAKE YOU THE HEAD AND NOT THE TAIL

abundant crops. He will open to you His wonderful treasury of rain in the heavens, to give you fine crops every season. He will bless everything you do; and you shall lend to many nations, but shall not borrow from them. If you will only listen and obey the commandments of the Lord your God that I am giving you today, He will make you the head and not the tail, and you shall always have the upper hand. But each of these blessings depends on your not turning aside in any way from the laws I have given you; and you must never worship other gods."[31] This promise was appropriate as Israel (Jacob and his descendants) truly were blessed when they moved to Egypt, and blessed again when they moved from Egypt.

When Moses penned these words, they were for Joshua to read aloud as all Israel made their pledge while on top of Mt. Gerizim. He knew these principles and was talking from experience. As all of Israel quoted from Deuteronomy 28, speaking of the promises of God, it is evident that God did bless them.

In the Sermon on the Mount, Jesus defined the Culture of the Kingdom by teaching wisdom to cope with the stresses and anxieties of life. He explained how we are not to worry about things like the food we need, the drink we consume and the clothes we wear. He said, "For you already have life and a body— and they are far more important than what to eat and wear. Look at the birds! They don't worry about what to eat—they don't need to sow or reap or store up food—for your heavenly Father feeds them. And you are far more valuable to him than they are. Will all your worries add a single moment to your life? And why worry about your clothes? Look at the field lilies; they don't worry about theirs. Yet King Solomon in all his glory was not clothed as beautifully as they. And if God cares so wonderfully for flowers that are here today and gone tomorrow, won't He more surely care for you, O men of little faith? So don't worry at all about having enough food and clothing. Why be like the heathen? For they take pride in all these things and are deeply concerned about them. But your heavenly Father already knows perfectly well that you need them, and He will give them to you if you give Him first place in your life and live as He wants you to. So don't be anxious about tomorrow. God will take care of your tomorrow too. Live one day at a time."[32]

The Nile River

The famine and all its ill effects continued to escalate throughout the region. Egypt had always placed much trust in the Nile, as being a supplier of nourishment for their agricultural needs. There were levels they always expected the Nile to rise to, but, "… it did not rise to its former heights, nor did God send rain upon it."[33]

The Nile River is the longest river in the world, and extends some 6,695 kilometers long (4,160 miles); it is generally a rushing torrent receiving its waters from both the White Nile and the Blue Nile. Egypt did not receive much rain at anytime, but far away in Ethiopia, where the Blue Nile had its origin there was always rain, except for these years of the great famine; and also the White Nile, which receives its water mostly from Lake Victoria, was not receiving rain. Therefore, the entire northeastern portion of Africa was cut off from rain for these years.

The Nile was, during this famine, running low in volume and much quieter in nature, because of such a shortage of rainfall.[34]

"The people had enjoyed the seven years of plenty, spending whatever they had for the moment with no thought or expectation that the future could be less productive. Of course they did not have the foresight that Pharaoh had; yet his foresight was to Joseph's credit."[35] No one in all of Egypt, made the least provision for themselves.

Endnotes

1. Josephus, Antiquities, Book 2, 7:2
2. Josephus, Antiquities, Book 2, 7:2
3. Josephus, Antiquities, Book 2, 7:3
4. Josephus, Antiquities, Book 2, 7:3
5. Genesis 46:1-7 TLB
6. Genesis 46:26-27 TLB
7. Genesis 46:28-29 NIV
8. Genesis 46:30 NKJV
9. Josephus, Antiquities, Book 2, 7:5
10. Genesis 46:31-34 MSG
11. Genesis 46:34 MSG
12. Genesis 46:34 NIV
13. Genesis 46:34 KJV
14. Genesis 43:32 KJV
15. Dake Bible, Genesis 46:34 page 47, "D"
16. Heliopolis was a suburb of modern Cairo in Lower Egypt
17. Genesis 47:1-6 TLB
18. Genesis 47:6 MSG
19. Paraphrased: Genesis 47:8
20. Genesis 47:9 NIV
21. Paraphrased: Genesis 47:12
22. Genesis 42:25
23. Genesis 42:24
24. Genesis 44:1-2
25. Genesis 45:18-23
26. Genesis 47:11-12
27. Exodus 12:40
28. Exodus 11:2-3; 12:35-36)
29. Exodus 16:13-15; Numbers 11:31
30. Deuteronomy 28:1-14 KJV
31. Deuteronomy 28:1-14 TLB
32. Matt. 6:25-34 TLB
33. Josephus, Antiquities, Book 2, 7:7
34. This annual flooding came to an end in the 1970s with the construction of the Aswan dam. Until the dam was built the breadbasket of Lower Egypt flooded and received nutrients, which made it excellent for farming. Today they use modern irrigation techniques.
35. Josephus, Antiquities, Book 2, 7:7

The Joseph Story

Chapter 15

THE FAMINE IS FINISHED— WHAT NOW?

T he governor, Zaphnath-paaneah, had the foresight to
prepare for this regional calamity, and the people of Egypt
were grateful.

As the years passed, the Egyptians noticed that more and more
of their family's budget was needed to purchase food. Eventually
there were no personal supplies of food, and even the money was
spent. "Joseph collected all the money that was to be found in
Egypt and Canaan to pay for the distribution of food. He banked
the money in Pharaoh's palace."[1]

"When the money of the people of Egypt and Canaan was
gone, all Egypt came to Joseph and said, 'Give us food, why
should we die before your eyes? Our money is used up.'"[2]

"Then bring your livestock," said Joseph. "I will sell you food
in exchange for your livestock, since your money is gone." So
they brought their livestock to Joseph, and he gave them food in
exchange for their horses, their sheep and goats, their cattle and

donkeys. And he brought them through that year with food in exchange for all their livestock."³

"The next year they came again and said, 'Our money is gone, and our cattle are yours, and there is nothing left but our bodies and land. Why should we die? Buy us, and our land, and we will be serfs to Pharaoh. We will trade ourselves for food, then we will live, and the land won't be abandoned.'"⁴

"Then Joseph bought all the land of Egypt for Pharaoh; for every man of the Egyptians sold his field, because the famine was severe upon them. So the land became Pharaoh's. And as for the people, he moved them into the cities from one end of the borders of Egypt to the other end."⁵

"Joseph made an exception for the priests. He didn't buy their land, because they received a fixed salary from Pharaoh and were able to live off of that salary. So they didn't need to sell their land."⁶

THE PEOPLE SAID "YOU HAVE SAVED OUR LIVES"

"Joseph said to the people, 'Now that I have bought you and your land today for Pharaoh, here is seed for you so you can plant the ground. But when the crop comes in, give a fifth of it to Pharaoh. The other four-fifths you may keep as seed for the fields and as food for yourselves and your households and your children.'"⁷

The people said, "You have saved our lives; let us find favor in the sight of my Lord, and we will be Pharaoh's servants. And Joseph made it a law over the land of Egypt to this day, that Pharaoh should have one-fifth, except for the land of the priests only, which did not become Pharaoh's."⁸

"Finally the famine ended and the misery ceased; the Nile River overflowed the ground, and the ground brought forth its fruits in abundance."[9] Once again the overflowing of the Nile River left deposits of rich dark soil and sediment on the land, creating fertile farmlands.

"This famine, in the end had brought upon the Egyptians not only starvation and calamity, but a personal loss of dignity.

They had struggled to survive and, in the end, had become slaves to Pharaoh, yielding up ownership to every material possession. In addition, they had lost their freedom to slavery."[10]

Joseph Gave Back their Freedom and Their Land

Egypt had progressed throughout the seven years of plenty. As landowners, they were financially strong. They were an agrarian culture. Essentially, as most nations of those days, they were not well educated. Superstition was a strong part of their national identity.

They had, however, emerged from the seven years of famine as a people grateful for their survival—even if it meant they had changed their national economy by becoming slaves to their king. Their money was finished. Their livestock belonged to Pharaoh and their land was no longer their own. Even their own flesh and human rights had been sold out just for the hope of living through the famine to the days when food would be available once again.

JOSEPH CONDUCTED "TOWN HALL MEETINGS" IN EACH DISTRICT

As a nation they had done what they had to do. Let the future take care of itself. For now, they had decided that they would accept their options and do what they must to keep themselves and their little ones alive.

At last it was over. The rains had begun to fall in far away places where the waters of the Nile were gathering. The future showed promise of returning to normal. They would do what was needed to rebuild Egypt back to its former glory.

God had given Joseph a plan to bless the Egyptians and to help them flourish again even after the famine. It seems that Joseph had put a lot of thought into this plan and that Pharaoh, who was like a son to Joseph,[11] had become a benevolent king. Here is the strategy, which is shown by Josephus as the way it was all handled after the famine.

"Joseph took a tour of all the lands of Egypt as the famine came to an end. After all, he was the one man who knew exactly how long it would last. He gathered the people in each city he visited; speaking to them about the land they had freely consented to relinquish to Pharaoh during the famine. He reminded them that, because of their agreement, Pharaoh was, in fact, the owner of these lands and possessed the right to farm the land and therefore to enjoy the fruit of the land himself."[12]

Joseph then, in an act of generosity, and speaking for Pharaoh, "… gave them back entirely the land."[13]

In conclusion, Joseph had done what he had to do to help the people get through this famine, but in the end gave them back the land, which had been seized by Pharaoh.

The men of Egypt were elated and, "… rejoiced upon their becoming, unexpectedly, owners of their lands, and diligently paid what tariff was required of them to give to Pharaoh."

JOSEPH ESTABLISHED A FLAT TAX OF TWENTY PERCENT IN EGYPT

The tax rate in Egypt became twenty percent. It was a flat tax and was linked directly to the harvest.

This was a law enacted by Joseph so that Pharaoh's government would have sufficient revenues to operate and to abound.[14]

The generosity shown by Joseph and by Pharaoh brought political dividends from the people. By taking care of business in this way, "… Joseph procured to himself a greater authority among the Egyptians, and greater love to the king from them."[15]

Endnotes

1. Genesis 47:14 MSG
2. Genesis 47:15 NIV
3. Genesis 47:16-17 NIV
4. Genesis 47:18-19 TLB
5. Genesis 47:20-21 NKJV
6. Genesis 47:22 MSG
7. Genesis 47:23-24 NIV
8. Genesis 47:25-26 NKJV
9. Paraphrased: Josephus, Antiquities, Book 2, 7:7
10. Paraphrased: Josephus, Antiquities, Book 2, 7:7
11. Genesis 45:8
12. Paraphrased: Josephus, Antiquities, Book 2, 7:7
13. Josephus, Antiquities, Book 2, 7:7
14. Genesis 47:26
15. Josephus, Antiquities, Book 2, 7:7

THE LAST DAYS OF THE MAIN MEN

"Israel settled down in Egypt in the region of Goshen. They acquired property and flourished. They became a large company of people. Jacob lived in Egypt for seventeen years. In all, he lived 147 years."[1]

From the days of Abraham great prosperity was a part of the lives of these Hebrews. Not only did they prosper, they enjoyed a veritable population explosion among them.[2] They acquired property and flourished.[3]

Jacob's days were quickly coming to a close. "As the time of his death drew near, he called for his son Joseph and said to him, 'If you are pleased with me, swear most solemnly that you will honor this, my last request: Do not bury me in Egypt. When I am dead, take me out of Egypt and bury me beside my ancestors.'"[4] Joseph gave his word that he would do as his father had asked. Soon afterwards Jacob took to his bed.[5]

Things settled into a normal routine as Joseph left his father's home in Goshen. Then word was brought to Joseph that his father was ill and his health was failing fast.

So Joseph took along with him, his two sons Manasseh and Ephraim and journeyed to Goshen to be with his father. "When Jacob was told, 'Your son Joseph has come to you,' Jacob rallied his strength and sat up on the bed."[6]

Jacob received Joseph and his two sons into his bedroom and immediately launched into a story from many years ago. He began to remind Joseph of the night when at Luz, as his head had laid upon a pillow of stone[7] the Lord God Almighty Himself had appeared to him in a dream. He shared with his son and two grandsons of how the Lord had blessed him and promised him, saying, "I will make you a great nation and I will give this land of Canaan to you and to your children's children, for an everlasting possession."[8]

JACOB HAD HOPE!

THE LORD HAD BEEN FAITHFUL TO HIM FROM THE BEGINNING

Jacob had always found great comfort (as well as a sense of value) when reflecting on the words God had given him in the past. He saw himself in light of his human failures and knew that he could not count for much if he did not have the grace of God at work in his life.

Each time he experienced a day of visitation from the Lord God, everything had changed. Jacob knew that the Lord was his hope. He had no hope without the Lord being at work in his life, his future, and his destiny.

This is the reason this elderly Patriarch declared with such power the words God had spoken to him in his earlier days.

Manasseh and Ephraim had entered the room with their father, Joseph, but as yet, had not been acknowledged by their feeble grandfather. Perhaps they wondered if he had even noticed their being present in the room.

Grace, Forgiveness, and Blessing

Between the paradigms of the carefree days of youth and the seriousness of adulthood, there is too often a great gulf. The young often struggle with ideas, purpose, ideals, and direction—even with insecurity. The older often struggle with personal insecurity, direction, ideas, purpose, and ideals. It is amazing how much common ground can be found.

The Holy Spirit begins a process of maturing in the lives of each succeeding generation. We often think ours is the only struggle, and yet these factors are common to all of mankind.

Sometimes the older generation will not pay enough attention to the younger one. Sometimes they prejudge them without hearing them out. In this story, the younger may have prejudged the older without realizing that Jacob was about to pay them a huge compliment and extend great favor by actually adopting them to become as his own sons.

The point to be taken here is a call for patience. Let us not be so quick to judge the motives of our friends and neighbors. Let us extend grace, forgiveness, and blessing in advance. Then if and when we are offended, let us display the grace, love, and forgiveness of our heavenly father by blessing instead of cursing.

Joseph's Two Sons are Adopted by Jacob

After his lengthy discourse, Jacob turned his full attention to speak of Joseph's two sons. He began to speak of his grandsons, Manasseh and Ephraim, with such love and care. Jacob spoke of how they had been born to Joseph during the time he was estranged from him and in this distant land of Egypt. You can almost hear the disappointment in his words that he had not been present on the days of their birth.

Jacob stiffened his back and moved into a more prophetic patriarchal mood by saying, "And now your two sons, Ephraim and Manasseh, who were born to you, in the land of Egypt ... they shall be mine."[9]

Joseph stood, with Manasseh and Ephraim, facing his father who was nearly blind. The boys had been so quiet that Jacob seemed not to even be aware that they were standing there.

Apparently, Jacob had been thinking about his grandsons for some time. Now that he was nearing the day of his death he felt that he had to take care of business. Upon establishing that many years earlier he had heard the voice of God, Jacob now declared that Joseph's two sons were that day moving from their rank as his grandsons to becoming his very own sons. He said, "I am adopting them..."[10] "Ephraim and Manasseh shall be as much mine as Reuben and Simeon."[11]

In effect these two grandsons became equal with the brothers of Joseph. It must be noticed however, that they will become known as each taking a half of the inheritance of Joseph (rather than an allotment given to Joseph as a tribe). This is a beautiful picture of how our descendants step in to pick up the valuable destiny and heritage which is passed on to them from their parents.[12]

There was never a tribe of Israel called by the name of "Joseph." Instead there were two half tribes: one known as the tribe of Ephraim, and the other known as Manasseh.

Jacob continued by addressing the position and rights of any future children which could be born to Joseph saying, "Joseph, you may go on to father more descendants, but those offspring will be my grandchildren, and will receive only the normal inheritance of the tribe of Joseph, which will come to them through the half tribes of Ephraim and Manasseh."[13]

Jacob concluded the ceremony by explaining his reasoning for giving special consideration of Joseph's two sons (Manasseh and Ephraim). He remembered that Rachel, his beloved and favorite wife, had died at an inconvenient time, outside of Bethlehem, while they were on a journey. In her death she had only given birth to two sons (Joseph and Benjamin). Rachel had delivered two sons even as Joseph had only fathered two sons. This aging patriarch felt that he had adequately addressed the troubling thoughts which he attached to Rachel and Joseph by granting special favor to these boys. Somehow, in all of this, Jacob felt closure and could finally allow Rachel to rest in peace.

With his business finished, Jacob now sensed the presence of Manasseh and Ephraim. He could faintly see the form of these two young men and asked Joseph, "Who are these?"[14]

IT IS ALWAYS BEST TO PRAY WITH YOUR EYES OPEN— AT LEAST, IF JACOB IS IN CHARGE

Joseph said to his father, "They are my sons, whom God has given me in this place." And Jacob said, "Please bring them to me, and I will bless them." Now the eyes of Jacob were dim with age, so that he could not see. Then Joseph brought them near him, and he kissed them and embraced them. And Jacob said to Joseph. "I had not thought to see your face; but in fact, God has shown me your offspring!"[15]

Joseph knew exactly what to do and pulled back the two boys. He bowed himself fully, with his head to the ground, he then repositioned his sons so that Ephraim would approach the patriarch to his left hand and Manasseh, the oldest, would be convenient to Jacob's right hand. "But Jacob crossed his arms as he stretched them out to lay his hands upon the boys' heads, so that his right hand was upon the head of Ephraim, the younger boy, and his left hand was upon the head of Manasseh, the older. He did this purposely."[16]

> "May the God before whom my fathers
>
> Abraham and Isaac walked,
>
> the God who has been my shepherd
>
> all my life to this day,
>
> the Angel who has delivered me from all harm
>
> may he bless these boys.
>
> May they be called by my name,
>
> and the names of my fathers, Abraham and Isaac,
>
> and may they increase greatly upon the earth."

Joseph was cherishing this moment and was in a private repose with his eyes, apparently closed, while listening to the pronouncements of his father, Jacob. Well into the prayer, Joseph looked up, perhaps opening one eye to observe the blessing of his firstborn, Manasseh, going mistakenly to his younger son. His adrenalin began to pump, and as if time stood still, he reached for the two hands of the Patriarch, almost wrestling them from the heads of his sons in an attempt to reposition them over the other.

Joseph tried very hard not to dishonor his father by accusing him, but said, "No, my father, this one is the firstborn; put your right hand on his head."[17] "But his father refused, 'I know what

I'm doing, my son.' He said, 'Manasseh too shall become a great nation, but his younger brother shall become even greater.'"[18]

Notice that each time Joseph spoke of his sons they were Manasseh and Ephraim, but each time Jacob spoke of them they were Ephraim and Manasseh. It is clear that in the mind of the aged patriarch, the "younger shall be greater than the older."

"The Elder Shall Serve the Younger"

Jacob had been born second to his twin brother, Esau. Even before their delivery, their mother Rebekah, had been aware that her "… children were fighting each other inside her! 'I can't endure this,' she exclaimed."[19]

Rebekah did the only thing she knew to do and fell to her knees to speak with the Lord.

> And the Lord said to her:
>
> "Two nations are in your womb,
>
> Two peoples shall be separated from your body;
>
> One people shall be stronger than the other,
>
> And the older shall serve the younger."[20]

Jacob, the younger (now 147 years later) was always the one to spot the leader. He always seemed to favor the opposite to what others would choose. He had enjoyed the benefits of the birthright even though the odds had been against him from the beginning. This is the same way it was as he had entered this world with this blessing. The prominent role would go to the younger. This defined his words of blessing in his two newest sons. They were Joseph's by Asenath, his wife, but now they would be Jacob's adopted sons; the second born would dominate all Israel as the largest of the tribes, and clearly more prominent than Manasseh.

YOU MUST BLESS YOUR DESCENDANTS

"On that day, Jacob moved into his final pronouncement and declared that from now on all of his descendants would pronounce blessings upon each other. They would say, 'May God make you like Ephraim and Manasseh.' And he set Ephraim before Manasseh."[21]

Jacob said to Joseph, "I am about to die, but God will be with you and take you back to the land of your fathers."[22]

"And beyond what I have given your brothers, I am giving you an extra portion of the land that I took from the Amorites with my sword and bow."[23]

Jacob's Last Words

Jacob called together all of his sons because he sensed that he must speak as a prophet to them. Many things had happened over the years. These sons had revealed their own hearts over and over again. Some of them had passed the tests of life and fulfilled their God-given assignments, while others had failed, faltered, and sinned greatly.

Joseph observed the clan as they gathered into the tent of their father—the great Patriarch, Israel (who had once been known only as Jacob). This man had once faltered in his own missteps, but a divine work of grace had rescued him and thrust him into a life which warranted a level of divine approval.

Once he had been the "seeker of blessing" from his patriarch father, Isaac. Now he was the "giver of blessing" to those who were his descendants. His sons gathered around for a closed meeting. Present were: Reuben, Simeon, Levi, Judah, Dan, Naphtali, Gad, Asher, Issachar, Zebulun, Joseph, and Benjamin.

THE FINAL
GATHERING
OF THE
"THE FAMILY"

Jacob's words began immediately and his addresses started with the eldest of his sons.

Reuben—First Born Son of Leah

Reuben did not fare well because of his moral failure during his youth. He had gone up to the bed of Bilhah (Rachel's maid) soon after the death of Rachel. Bilhah had become Jacob's third wife after Leah and Rachel, but now had been defiled by the sin of incest. In Jacob's final words he had nothing of blessing for his oldest son, Reuben. He should have, and indeed he could have received double honor by being Jacob's firstborn, but instead he found himself dishonored because of the sins of his youth.[24] Jacob declared Reuben to be as "unstable as water."[25]

Simeon and Levi—Second and Third Born Sons of Leah

The second and third born sons of Leah also found themselves facing the condemnation of their father because of horrific crimes they had committed against a neighboring village in Canaan.[26] Simeon and Levi had brought great shame and embarrassment to the entire family. As a result, they all had to move away from that area, relocating to Bethel.[27] When Jacob was searching for a blessing, he could not find one. The descendants of Simeon and Levi would not receive a proper division of land when all of the Hebrews would exodus from Egypt, but would, instead, be assigned to scattered cities within the lands, which would belong to their fellow tribesmen.

Judah—Fourth Born Son of Leah

Judah was the first son to receive a proper blessing on that day from the mouth of the patriarch. Jacob declared that Judah would prosper, and would triumph over his enemies. He is reckoned as the one from whom the Messiah himself would come. Jacob spoke of a royal line and how, "the scepter shall not depart from Judah until the Messiah comes."[28] It was declared by Jacob that Judah would receive a major part of the ruling side of the Patriarchal blessing, just as Joseph would receive the actual birthright.[29]

Zebulun—Fifth Born Son of Leah

Jacob spoke to Zebulun and told him that what he could see in him was the inclination to live by the sea. He told him that his descendants would command the seashores and provide a haven for those who lived on the sea and were involved in the shipping industry.[30]

Issachar—Sixth Born Son of Leah

Issachar would have a gentle and compliant nature. This would, however, render him susceptible to those who would like to take advantage of him.[31] Too often he would be forced to pay tribute and taxes because of his nature.

Dan—First Born Son of Bilhah (Rachel's Maid)

Dan would assume oversight of his own destiny. Jacob could see right into the nature of Dan and how he had an intuitive ability to discern the unjust motives of men.

Gad—First Born Son of Zilpah (Leah's Maid)

Gad will be attacked by bandits and robbers. However, it will become clear that it is not wise to become an enemy of Gad, for he will prove to be up to the challenge.[32] Those who would have ill intentions against Gad should be careful because the men of Gad will defeat them in the end.

Asher—Second Born Son of Zilpah (Leah's Maid)

Asher would become famous for his skill in preparing excellent foods, pastries, and dainties fit for kings.[33]

Naphtali—Second Born Son of Bilhah (Rachel's Maid)

"Naphtali is a deer running free that gives birth to lovely fawns."[34] Jacob saw Naphtali and his descendants as being poetic and free spirited.

Joseph—First Born Son of Rachel

Jacob praised Joseph, describing him as a fruitful tree which flourished, having taken root beside a fountain. This, of course, confirms that Joseph's depth of faith in God is best seen as waters which run deeply. He was portrayed as one who would not be held back by difficult trials or circumstance, but would actually scale the wall that would attempt to hold him back.[35] "The archers with malice attacked, shooting their hate-tipped arrows; but he held steady under fire, his bow firm, his arms limber, with the backing of the Champion of Jacob, the Shepherd, and the Rock of Israel."[36]

It must be considered that Jacob's comment about the "hate-tipped arrows" may be his way of referring to how the brothers sold him into slavery.

Benjamin—Second Born Son of Rachel

Finally Jacob turned his comments to speak prophetically and with insight into the root nature of Benjamin. He spoke these strange words: "Benjamin is a ravenous wolf, in the morning devouring the prey and at night dividing the spoil."[37]

"The tribe of Benjamin was absorbed by the tribe of Judah and is not mentioned after the return from the Babylonian captivity, except in connection with its former land, or as the home tribe of some individual person."[38] Some of these men were Ehud, the Judge; King Saul, Israel's first king; Jonathan, the prince, son of King Saul; and the Apostle Paul, otherwise known as Saul of Tarsus.

Final Instructions

Jacob had spoken honestly and candidly to the destiny and nature of each of his sons. He did not like all that he had to say, but he spoke the truth as he saw it after many years of observation.

Jacob gave final instructions to his sons, telling them clearly that in a few minutes he would actually die and be gathered to his ancestors. Very clearly he articulated the place he wished them to transport him to for burial. His burial must be in Canaan, in a cave located on property which had been purchased by Abraham from a Hittite by the name of Ephron. This cave was the burial site for Abraham and Sarah, as well as Isaac and his wife, Rebekah. Jacob added, "I also buried Leah there."[39]

"Jacob finished instructing his sons, pulled his feet into bed, breathed his last, and was gathered to his people."[40]

"Joseph threw himself upon his father's body and wept over him and kissed him. Afterwards he commanded his morticians to embalm the body."[41] After the required period of national mourning of seventy days, Pharaoh gave Joseph leave to travel to the chosen burial site in Canaan. Many Egyptian dignitaries, and "… senior officers of the land, as well as all of Joseph's people—his brothers and their families,"[42] traveled together in a large procession to the cave at Mamre in Canaan. "But they left their little children and flocks and herds in the land of Goshen. So a very great number of chariots, cavalry, and people accompanied Joseph."[43]

"Arriving at the Atad Threshing Floor just across the Jordan River, they stopped for a period of mourning, letting their grief out in loud and lengthy lament. For seven days, Joseph engaged in these funeral rites for his father."

"When the Canaanites who lived in that area saw the grief being poured out at the Atad Threshing Floor, they said, 'Look how deeply the Egyptians are mourning.'"[44]

"Jacob's sons continued to carry out his instructions to the letter. They took him on into Canaan and buried him in the cave in the field of Machpelah facing Mamre, the field that Abraham had bought as a burial plot from Ephron the Hittite."[45]

The funeral was over and the burial rites finished; so Joseph, his family, and all the guests returned to Egypt, to their homes and to their families.

Joseph's brothers began to consider that their father had been their protector in life, but now was not there to protect them should Joseph decide to repay them for all the evil they had done to him. Guilt and fear began to take over in their hearts as they began to evaluate their own future.[46]

Did Jacob Ever Know?

It seems very clear that Jacob was finally aware of all the sins committed against Joseph by his ten older sons. After the death of Jacob they quoted Jacob's instruction that Joseph must fully forgive his brothers for the treachery they had committed against him those thirty-nine years earlier.[47]

Jacob's ten sons sent a message to Joseph informing him that their father had left them with instructions regarding the need to avoid retaliation. They said, "Your father left these instructions before he died: This is what you are to say to Joseph: I ask you to forgive your brothers the sins and the wrongs they committed in treating you so badly. Now please forgive the sins of the servants of the God of your father."[48]

"When Joseph read the message, he broke down and cried. Then his brothers came and fell down before him and said, 'We are your slaves!' But Joseph told them, 'Don't be afraid of me. Am I God, to judge and punish you? As far as I am concerned, God turned into good what you meant for evil, for he brought me to this high position I have today so that I could save the lives of many people. No, don't be afraid. Indeed, I myself will take care of you and your families.' And he spoke very kindly to them, reassuring them."[49]

Guilt is a terrible force. It arrives in the heart of an individual without warning and disables a life from moving forward. Guilt can imprison hopes and dreams and drive its victim to failure and even death.

GUILT CAN ONLY THRIVE WHERE THERE IS AN ABSENCE OF GRACE

These brothers of Joseph had heard him express forgiveness with their ears, but the Old Testament law was void of the honest grace which was available in the New Testament. They found themselves paralyzed after the death of their father. They could only guess that Joseph was made of the same stuff they had been made of those thirty-nine years before.

It seems that this outburst from his brothers was the final test of grace and forgiveness which Joseph would endure. After he successfully "reassured them, speaking with them heart-to-heart,"[50] they were finally able to put their fears to rest, forgetting their suspicions.

JACOB LIVED 17 YEARS IN EGYPT, PASSING AWAY AT THE AGE OF 147

JOSEPH WAS 39 YEARS OLD WHEN HE HAD HIS REUNION WITH JACOB AFTER 22 YEARS OF BEING AWAY FROM HIS FAMILY

JOSEPH WAS AGE 56 WHEN HIS FATHER PASSED

JOSEPH LIVED 54 MORE YEARS TO DIE AT 110

Joseph "lived to see Ephraim's sons into the third generation. The sons of Makir, Manasseh's son, were also recognized as Joseph's."[51]

"Soon I will die," Joseph told his brothers, "but God will surely come and get you, and bring you out of this land of Egypt and take you back to the land he promised to the descendants of Abraham, Isaac, and Jacob. Then Joseph made his brothers promise with an oath that they would take his body back with them when they returned to Canaan. So Joseph died at the age of 110, and they embalmed him, and his body was placed in a coffin in Egypt."[52]

A Man of Faith

Joseph was truly a man of faith. In Hebrews 11:22 the writer of Hebrews states a fact regarding Joseph saying, "By an act of faith, Joseph, while dying, prophesied the exodus of Israel, and made arrangements for his own burial."[53]

Faith enables the believer to see beyond the present circumstances to define the next step even though their own consciousness is about to slip away for a moment. Faith in our eternal hope enables us to grasp eternity ... the eternity which is just beyond the horizon and only moments away.

~ The End ~

Endnotes

1. Genesis 47: 28 MSG
2. Genesis 47:27 TLB
3. Genesis 47:27 MSG
4. Genesis 47:29-31 NLT
5. Genesis 47: 31 TLB
6. Genesis 48:1-2 NIV
7. Genesis 28:11-19
8. Genesis 48:4 TLB
9. Genesis 48:5 AMP
10. Genesis 48:5 AMP
11. Genesis 48:5 NJB
12. A thought to consider: Joseph's brothers had been jealous because he, at age 17, had been promoted, with the birthright, over them. Now their nephews, Joseph's sons, were being elevated to the same level as they were, even though they were grandsons, and not actually Jacob's sons. Note, however, that Manasseh and Ephraim each received only half of Joseph's inheritance.
13. Genesis 48:6
14. Genesis 48:8 KJV
15. Genesis 48:9-11 NKJV
16. Genesis 48:12-14 TLB
17. Genesis 48:18 NIV
18. Genesis 48:19 TLB
19. Genesis 25:22 TLB
20. Genesis 25:23 NKJV
21. Genesis 48:20 AMP
22. Genesis 48:21-22 NIV
23. Genesis 48:22 NLT
24. History has produced many leaders who, because of personal failures, have been profoundly disappointed with the epitaph, which defined their lives.
25. Genesis 49:4 KJV
26. Genesis 34
27. Genesis 35:1
28. Genesis 49:10
29. I Chronicles 5:1-2
30. Genesis 49:13 NIV
31. Genesis 49:14-15
32. Genesis 49:19
33. Genesis 49:20 MSG
34. Genesis 49:21 MSG
35. Paraphrased: Genesis 49:22
36. Genesis 49:23-24 MSG
37. Genesis 49:27 AMP

38. Notes from: King James Version/Amplified Bible, Parallel Edition, copyright 1995, by the Zondervan Corporation and the Lockman Foundation, Page 73
39. Genesis 49:29-32
40. Genesis 49:33 MSG
41. Genesis 50:1-2 TLB
42. Genesis 50:2-8 TLB
43. Genesis 50:8-9 TLB
44. Genesis 50:10-11 MSG
45. Genesis 50:1-13 MSG
46. Genesis 50:15
47. Paraphrased: Genesis 50:16-17
48. Genesis 50:16-17 NIV
49. Genesis 50:17-21 TLB
50. Genesis 50:21 MSG
51. Genesis 50:22-23 MSG
52. Genesis 50:24-26 TLB
53. Hebrews 11:22 MSG

THE JOSEPH STORY IN REVIEW

This section of the book will provide you with more interesting facts and life lessons that can be learned from the story of Joseph. Included in this Appendix are the following sections:

Scripture Affirms the Story of Joseph

The Three Coats of Joseph:

- **The First Coat—Joseph's Coat from Jacob**
- **The World of "In Between Chapters"**
- **The Second Coat—Joseph's Coat from Potiphar**
- **The Third Coat—Joseph's Coat from Pharoah**

The Joseph Story

SCRIPTURE AFFIRMS THE STORY OF JOSEPH

Psalm 105:7-22 MSG

He's God, our God,

    in charge of the whole earth.

And he remembers, remembers his Covenant— for a

    thousand generations he's been as good as his word.

It's the Covenant he made with Abraham,

    the same oath he swore to Isaac,

The very statute he established with Jacob,

    the eternal Covenant with Israel,

Namely, "I give you the land.

    Canaan is your hill-country inheritance."

When they didn't count for much,
 a mere handful, and strangers at that,
Wandering from country to country,
 drifting from pillar to post,
He permitted no one to abuse them.
 He told kings to keep their hands off:
"Don't you dare lay a hand on my anointed,
 don't hurt a hair on the heads of my prophets."
Then he called down a famine on the country,
 he broke every last blade of wheat.
But he sent a man on ahead:
 Joseph, sold as a slave.
They put cruel chains on his ankles,
 an iron collar around his neck,
Until God's word came to the Pharaoh,
 and God confirmed his promise.
God sent the king to release him.
 The Pharaoh set Joseph free;
He appointed him master of his palace,
 put him in charge of all his business
To personally instruct his princes
 and train his advisors in wisdom.

Appendix

THE THREE COATS OF JOSEPH

The Joseph Story

JOSEPH'S COAT FROM JACOB

Principles Learned from Joseph's First Coat

Joseph's First Coat came from Jacob, his father, the patriarch.

- He chose Joseph to be the Prince, and gave him a robe of honor.

- The coat was colorful, regal and brilliant, and could be described as:

  - Youthful

  - Ethnic

  - Expressive

Joseph's first coat reflected the future favor, which was to come to him.

- ❧ At this early point in Joseph's history,
  his favor came from his father.

- ❧ In the future favor would come, from God,
  government officials, and finally from his family.

Who owned this brilliant coat?

- ❧ This coat was given to Joseph, but because of
  his youth it would still belong to Jacob, even
  though Joseph thought it was his own.

- ❧ In the Bible days, children became adults at age thirty.

- ❧ "Let me show you the implications of this. As long
  as the heir is a minor, he has no advantage over the
  slave. Though legally he owns the entire inheritance,
  he is subject to tutors and administrators until
  whatever date the father has set for emancipation."[1]

- ❧ Therefore, both Joseph and the coat
  itself were part of Jacob's assets.

- ❧ In reality, Joseph owned nothing, until the day he
  would be recognized as a man—age thirty.

- ❧ In essence, the first coat was a promise
  of great things to come.

Lessons for the young:

- Your first coat must be held loosely, because you are too young to truly appreciate its value and its significance.

- Life is a learning experience and many changes occur in early adulthood. An example is popularity in high school, which often does not translate into success as an adult.

- Keep in mind that, what is not yours, can be easily taken from you, because you cannot be assured that it will be protected against loss.

This coat is a picture lesson for us.

- It shows just how careful we all must be when it comes to what is placed into our hands.

- It is so easy to take for granted our right of ownership.

- It is easy to think we *deserve* the benefits which are coming our way.

- Do you have a truly thankful heart for the many benefits, which you have received?

Pay attention—where is your focus?

- It is easy to focus too much on the permanence of the first coat, when, in fact, there may be more and better coats in your future, as there will be more "life chapters."

- Life is full of hidden messages of wisdom

- If you will pay attention, you will avoid a host of disappointments.

Jacob gave to Joseph his first coat. It should have had written *Disclaimers*, or even a *Warning Label*, sown on the inside of it. These disclaimers might have gone something like this:

Wearing this coat could shorten your life:

- This coat represents a chapter in your life.

- You will be tested if you dare be so bold as to wear it.

- This coat is not permanent. It represents your first experience of significance.

- If you spread the wearing of this coat out to only 2-3 times a week, then you may avoid inciting the anger of the envious a bit longer.

- If you wear it every waking moment, then you may find it angers those who tend to get jealous.

Do not button this coat:

- Always wear it loosely

- The tighter you wear it, the more difficult it will be to remove it from your body, thus the greater the danger of injury to your person.

- If you button this coat, your wounds will be more severe; therefore, refrain from buttoning it.

- Leave your future in God's hands, so you will not be disappointed.

Do not get attached to this coat:

- Do not be deceived: This coat really isn't yours to keep.

- Youth is temporary and fleeting.

- It is likely that you will only be the steward of this coat a short time.

- Don't get too comfortable with your surroundings. God has BIGGER PLANS for you.

- If you get too comfortable with your newfound favor and take it for granted, then beware; it could be taken from you.

- Most lives have more than one chapter. If this is your first chapter, then you must realize that there will be more life chapters to come.

Enjoy it while it lasts:

- Note: If this coat represents your first major break, or "your first exciting life chapter," then you are served notice that: your "true and lasting coat of destiny" will probably not come until you have lived through a few more "life chapters."

- Therefore, just go ahead and wear this coat out... enjoy it while it lasts, because you'll have to go through a few "hard knocks" in life before you really get to own your own coat.

This coat is only a hint of what the real coat will be like

- This coat is a promise, a hint, and a shadow
of the truly great things to come.

- It'll be worth the wait, so be patient, and take your
hits realizing that everything is a process.

- Remember, don't take yourself too seriously, but remain
humble and able to laugh out loud whenever possible.

Endnotes

1. Galatians 4:1 MSG

THE WORLD OF "IN BETWEEN CHAPTERS"

When you enter a gray area, which is tucked between the major events of your life, it is a different life chapter all in itself. Joseph's journey from Canaan to Egypt was almost surreal. A bit like entering the twilight zone,[1] it was very different from his past, and would prove to be completely different from his future. His memory gave him a focus on his life in Canaan, but he could not begin to guess what his future would be like in the land which lay ahead.

Joseph was being pulled along the sandy pathway by the ropes that bound him. He could see little more than the rear end of the camel which he followed. It is likely that a loincloth was the only clothing to cover his nakedness.

The best way to reflect what this "in between chapter" is like is to say that Joseph went naked from one chapter to the next. Joseph had two "in between chapters:"

- ❧ Twilight Zone # 1 – His journey from Canaan to Egypt
- ❧ Twilight Zone # 2 – His time spent in Potiphar's Prison

Total loss is a difficult place to be. Many people experience a time of having lost virtually everything. Failure and disappointment may grip you as you loose your hold on status, marriage, assets, vocation, and reputation. Your reality may be that you are broken in every way possible and you are left with a sandcastle ready to be totally washed away by the next wave. In such times you can discover that the Holy Spirit is not only one who can help build your life, but also one who can help "rebuild" your life—restoring all that has been lost.

The desire of every human being is that life should be a natural progression which takes us always forward and upward. Altercations and detours are generally not enjoyed, but only tolerated. We wish for success to follow hope and good times to introduce even happier times. Life sometimes brings you to a lull, a down moment, or a state of total bewilderment like the look of the deer caught in the headlamps of an oncoming truck. It is a challenge when we are stripped or disgraced, broken or bankrupt, empty and without answers.

If you find yourself in such a place of awkward transition, just remember this: Don't think your life has come to an end if you are, like Joseph, in the world of "in between chapters." Allow your faith to rise to a higher level. Put your trust in God to bring you out of this valley and gracefully into your next assignment. You have finished one chapter and are poised and waiting for what is coming next. Keep this in mind: there is life after loss. Remind yourself of these statements:

- ❋ "Joseph knew that his dreams were RIGHT.

- ❋ He knew that his dreams were REAL.

- ❋ He knew that God was still on the throne,

- ❋ And that God would bring his dreams to pass."[2]

Endnotes

1. The term "Twilight Zone" simply refers to a "gray area." It has also been seen as the border between "night and day" on a planetary body. Wikipedia

2. I heard Zig Ziglar say this in a speech in a live talk. Zig Ziglar Corporate Headquarters, 5055 West Park Boulevard, Suite 700, Plano, TX 75093

The Joseph Story

JOSEPH'S COAT FROM POTIPHAR

Principles Learned from Joseph's Second Coat

Potiphar was one of Egypt's Supreme Officers:

- Chief of Police

- Captain of the Personal Body Guard of Pharaoh

- Egypt's Chief Executioner

Potiphar was handpicked by the Lord to make the purchase:

- He saw gifts and abilities in Joseph

- He paid the price and purchased this slave

He gave to Joseph a coat, which was a good fit for his assignment:

- **Joseph's Assignment:**
  - He was the personal aide of Egypt's most powerful bureaucrat.
  - He must see to details for a perfectionist.
  - He must manage state dinners, political friends, purchase of household supplies, oversee the agricultural and business interests as well as social events, and be, of course, the Director of Human Resources. (Joseph must do all this while still balancing the reality that he himself was a slave.)
  - Joseph was an asset of Egypt and not a citizen.

Joseph needed all the help he could get:

- Potiphar's tailor had a "power suit" designed for Joseph to wear—with all the culture and style necessary to make statements (when statements must be made).

- Joseph's second coat, reflected just the right touch of authority, confidence, and image.

- Joseph was, after all, the concierge of one of Egypt's most significant palatial homes.

JOSEPH AND THIS "SECOND COAT" ARE THE PROPERTY OF POTIPHAR—HIS SLAVE MASTER

- Joseph was the personal assistant to this very powerful Egyptian, Potiphar.

- In these circles, and with this coat, Joseph was, "The Man."

The coat give to Joseph by Potiphar should have had written *Disclaimers*, or even a *Warning Label*! These disclaimers might have gone something like this:

Wearing this coat could be harmful to your health:

- You have a high position and you look good wearing this coat.

- Be careful of those around you who have an agenda to ensnare you.

- You live in a world of competitive politics— conventional wisdom says, "Watch your back."

Do not button this coat:

- On a good day, it's okay to button this coat, but if it is a bad day then you'll wish it were unbuttoned, so you could easily make your escape.

- The challenge is to know if today is a good day or a bad day.

- One bit of advice: Keep a close eye on your moral character. Don't slip up.

Do not get attached to this coat:

- This coat will increase your confidence level, but remember that you and your coat are not one.

- This coat does not reflect WHO YOU REALLY ARE.

- You are more than the sum total of this coat and all it represents.

- Believe it or not, even if this coat fits you well, you are a bigger man than this coat was made for.

Enjoy it while it lasts:

- Note: If this coat is either your first, or second coat, you should prepare yourself for the day you have it no more.

- Life is generally a process of growing from one level to another, all the while gaining agility and insight as you navigate through mine fields, piranhas in the market place or ministry, and relationships.

- So, as for the coat, enjoy it while it lasts.

- Remember, if you hold this coat too closely, or if you walk with it tightly buttoned, then you may be pulled into situations, which become distasteful.

This coat is only a hint of what the real coat will be like:

- This coat is almost as good as it gets, but only God knows how good it can really get.

- God is your Creator and the personal designer of every man's destiny including yours—the wearer of this coat.

* Stay on alert, remain vigilant, and don't get too carried away with this chapter of your life.

* Expect great things from God for your future.

* Your next coat may be yours to keep.

Endnotes ———————————————————————

1. The term "Twilight Zone" simply refers to a "gray area." It has also been seen as the border between "night and day" on a planetary body. Wikipedia
2. Psalm 75:6-7

JOSEPH'S COAT FROM PHARAOH

Principles Learned from Joseph's Third Coat

- Pharaoh was Egypt's supreme ruler, their king.
- He was considered Egypt's highest life form and even a god.
- His judgment was final.

- Pharaoh chose Joseph to stand beside him.
- Pharaoh knew his own limitations, but was not insecure.

- He selected Joseph to be sworn in as Prime Minister.

- He believed in and trusted Joseph's judgment.
- He recognized Joseph's ability to hear from God.

- Pharaoh gave Joseph total authority over all Egypt.
- By this authority he was now a FREE MAN—no longer a slave.

- Pharaoh gave Joseph the signet ring of "Power" from his own finger.
- He gave Joseph a coat (Joseph's third coat). He gave him better than a coat...
  - It was a robe of fine linen.
  - This robe was fit only for a king.
  - It was a robe of such beauty that all would stop, bow, and behold it wide eyed.

- The robe Joseph now wore was absolutely the best that any earthly kingdom could give.
- Joseph was now a man ... he was 30 years old.
- This coat was the coat of "fulfilled promises."
- This coat was the symbol of fulfilled prophecies and night visions.
- Truly this coat was "as good as it gets" in this world.

- Who owned this coat? Joseph.
- Who could take this coat from him? No One.
- This coat did not need to come with a WARNING LABEL, because he had built the right character into his life, and this was "Joseph's hour."

- Joseph had passed all the tests and trials which had come his way.

- Joseph was now able to walk in his destiny.

- He had become the man whom God had wanted him to be.

- While wearing this coat, this time would prove to be Joseph's finest hour.

The Joseph Story

AMP—The Amplified Bible

Scripture quotations taken from the Amplified® Bible, Copyright © 1954, 1958, 1962, 1964, 1965, 1987 by The Lockman Foundation. La Habra, CA. Used by permission.

CEV—Contemporary English Version

Scripture quotations taken from the Contemporary English Version ®, Copyright © 1995 American Bible Society. All rights reserved.

KJV—King James Version

Scripture taken from the King James Version of the Bible®, Copyright © 1982 by Broadman & Holman Publishers, Nashville, TN. Used by permission. All rights reserved.

MSG—The Message

Scripture taken from The Message®. Copyright © 1993, 1994, 1995, 1996, 2000, 2001, 2002. Used by permission of NavPress Publishing Group. Colorado Springs, CO. All rights reserved.

NASB—New American Standard Bible

Scripture quotations taken from the New American Standard Bible®, Copyright © 1960, 1962, 1963, 1968, 1971, 1972, 1973, 1975, 1977, 1995 by The Lockman Foundation. Used by permission.

NIV—New International Version

Scripture taken from the HOLY BIBLE, NEW
INTERNATIONAL VERSION ®. Copyright © 1973, 1978,
1984 Biblica. Used by permission of Zondervan. All rights
reserved.

NKJV—New King James Version

Scripture taken from the New King James Version (NKJV) of
the Bible. Copyright © 1982 by Thomas Nelson, Inc. Used by
permission. All rights reserved.

NLT—New Living Translation

Scripture quotations are taken from the Holy Bible, New
Living Translation, copyright 1996, 2004. Used by permission
of Tyndale House Publishers, Inc., Wheaton, Illinois 60189. All
rights reserved.

TJB—The Jerusalem Bible

Scripture taken from The Jerusalem Bible. Copyright © 1966,
1967, 1968. Darton, Longman & Todd Ltd. and Doubleday &
Company, Inc. All rights reserved.

TLB—The Living Bible

Scrpture taken from The Living Bible. Copyright © 1987 by
Tyndale House Publishers, Inc., Wheaton, Illinois 60189. All
rights reserved.

The Life and Works of Flavius Josephus, Complete and Unabridged. Translated by William Whiston, A.M., Published by: Hendrickson Publishers, Peabody, MA 01961, Copyright © 1987

Dakes' Annotated Reference Bible, by Finis Jennings Dake, Published by Dake Bible Sales, Inc., PO Box 1050, Lawrenceville, GA 30246, Copyright © 1963.

Rick Warren's The Purpose Driven Life, Appendix 3, page 325 Zondervan, Grand Rapids, MI 49530 Copyright © 2002.

Zig Zigler Corporate Headquarters, 5055 West Park Boulevard, Suite 700, Plano, TX 75093.

Notes

Notes

Notes

Notes

Notes